INCREDIBLE
ANSWERS TO
PRAYER

INCREDIBLE ANSWERS TO PRAYER

Roger Morneau

REVIEW AND HERALD® PUBLISHING ASSOCIATION
WASHINGTON, DC 20039-0555
HAGERSTOWN, MD 21740

This book was
Edited by Gerald Wheeler
Designed by Bill Kirstein
Cover art by © Hans Wendler/The Image Bank
Type set: 10 pt. Novarese Medium

PRINTED IN U.S.A.

94 93 92   10 9 8 7 6 5

Library of Congress Cataloging in Publication Data

Morneau, Roger J., 1925-
    Incredible answers to prayer / Roger Morneau.
        p.   cm.
    1. Prayer. 2. Morneau, Roger J., 1925-   I. Title.
BV220.M67   1990   89-29263
248.3'2—dc20   CIP

ISBN 0-8280-0530-3

Contents

DEDICATION

This book is dedicated to my grandchildren, whom I love very much. While my pilgrimage through this land of the enemy is coming to a close, theirs is just beginning. My concern for their well-being in this present life, and through the eternal ages, weighs heavily upon my heart. Therefore, I have recorded in this volume some of the many outworkings of God's Holy Spirit in my behalf during the past sixty-plus years of my life, in the hope that here they will find encouragement in the Lord and the inspiration that will help them develop a living faith—a faith that will increase their spiritual strength and develop an unfaltering trust in our heavenly Father, and in the power of His Holy Spirit.

Most of the names in this book have been changed to protect the privacy of those involved in the events depicted.

CHAPTER
1

This Is the House of Death

On December 1, 1984, I was on the verge of dying in the intensive care unit of the Greater Niagara General Hospital in Niagara Falls, Ontario. I had congestive heart failure and atrial fibrillation that the physicians could not reverse. As the cardiologist stated a few days later, if my wife had taken 20 minutes longer in getting me to the hospital, I would have been dead before arrival.

It came upon me unexpectedly. My wife, Hilda, and I were visiting her mother for the weekend. Our trip from central New York had been pleasant, and we had had an enjoyable evening with Mother. Retiring at 10:00 p.m., I felt unusually tired and slept comfortably till about 3:00 a.m., when I awoke with sweat pouring down my face. Although I realized that I was having some discomfort in breathing, I attributed it to the bedroom being overheated.

When I opened the window about two inches, the cool winter air immediately improved my condition. However, I could not get back to sleep. I kept tossing in bed, and my breathing problem returned after a while.

I kept opening the window wider as breathing became more difficult, till by 7:00 a.m. I had it completely up.

After taking a shower, I became extremely tired and realized that something was definitely wrong with me. It took all the strength I could muster just to shave. Walking to the car required as much effort as if I were climbing a hill.

In the emergency room the staff quickly rigged me up with an oxygen mask, intravenous tubing dripping medication into my system, and a diagnostic monitor to check the activities of my heart. A cardiologist with the assistance of several nurses did everything that they could to keep me alive.

A short while later they placed me in the intensive care unit which was already filled to capacity. Because all the glassed-in chambers were occupied, they assigned me a bed in the open area close to the nurses' station.

I had, so to speak, a foot already in the grave, as my breathing had grown so shallow that I could hardly get any oxygen into my lungs. I now believed that I was going to die, and my conviction deepened when someone asked if I would like to have a minister come and see me. In my feeble condition I stated that I felt too sick to have anyone visit, except my wife, who was allowed to see me for 10 minutes every two hours. Besides, for almost 40 years I had made it a daily practice to seek out God and prepare myself to die.

Nearly four decades before, I had had the unique experience of having demonic spirits declare that I would go to an early grave because I had decided to accept Christ Jesus as my Lord and Saviour and to observe the biblical Sabbath. (See my previous book, A *Trip Into the Supernatural* [Review and Herald, 1982], where I recount my unusual story.)

While I realized that my condition was critical, I was also aware that a number of other people in the ward were struggling to hold on to life. "This is the house of death," I told myself.

The Presence of God

Thirty-six hours passed, and I was still alive and now able to breathe without having the oxygen mask on all the time. My thoughts ascended to God in a melody of praise.

That Sunday evening the intensive care unit was in a state of great urgency, and the head nurse called for additional help to meet the situation. To my immediate right an elderly man appeared on the point of death as two nurses struggled to keep him alive. To my left, a man in his 30s, already having had three heart attacks, stated that he was probably living his last days.

Lights flashed at the nurses' station with increasing frequency as the condition of a great number of patients worsened. Because of my close proximity to the station, I could hear comments that indicated that the condition of some patients was deteriorating and becoming desperate. Considering the situation, I recalled something that a leading spiritist had said in 1946. He stated that demonic spirits delight in seeing people die, and in times of war they celebrate. Clearly they would be planning such a celebration that very evening with so many patients in the ICU so near death.

Not for myself, but for others, my thoughts ascended to God in prayer. For 39 years I had seen the power of intercessory prayer bring great blessings into the lives of many. One practice that I had formed early in my Christian life was to bring the spiritually sick, those who have had head-on collisions with sin and become spiritual and at times physical wrecks, to what I like to refer to as Christ's intensive care unit. The results had been rewarding, as many times I had seen my prayers answered before my eyes.

As I considered my Lord and Saviour in the Holy of Holies of the heavenly sanctuary ministering in behalf of fallen humanity (Hebrews 8:1, 2), I found my heart soaring in thanksgiving for all the many blessings He had so compassionately bestowed others in answer to my prayers. And my joy in the Lord was great as I reflected upon God's never failing compassion toward me a most undeserving human being.

Now I asked for the mighty power of the Holy Spirit of God to surround everyone with a spiritual atmosphere of light and peace and to restore them to health if it was His will. As you will see in later chapters, I had learned through personal experience that intercessory prayers are most effective when I have made sure that sin is not separating the subjects of my prayers from God. I began my prayers in that intensive care unit by thanking God for the privilege of asking for His divine help for my fellow patients. Pointing to the infinite price He had paid at Calvary, I asked Him to forgive everyone's sins.

For a long time it has been my conviction that as Christians we ought to do for others what they cannot or are unwilling to do for themselves—to deal with the sin in their lives. Jesus set the example for us. As He died on the cross, He asked the Father to forgive the sins of those who crucified Him (Luke 23:34). I cannot explain what happens when we ask God to forgive the sins of another, but I have seen the transformations that begin taking place in his or her life. God never violates the free will of anyone, but when we pray for someone else, it permits Him to work in lives with a special power. He unshackles the individual from the chains of sin so that he can use his freedom of choice to choose good.

And to encourage my own Christian experience as I lay at the point of death, I asked God to allow me to see His healing touch at work in that ICU. Then I thanked the Great Physician, the Author of our being, for answering my prayers.

As I had discovered years before, demonic spirits struggle hard before yielding their prey to the power of the Spirit of God. For about 15 minutes a large number of patients experienced increasing distress, and nurses actually ran to their aid. Then the medical staff's fears became reality as the heart of a Mr. Smith stopped beating.

The emergency beeper at the nursing station went into action, intensifying the sense of urgency. Immediately the head nurse asked over the PA system for all the doctors in the hospital to come and assist. Three physicians raced into the unit. A nurse on the run retrieved the resuscitator that had been left at the opposite end of the room.

About 10 minutes went by while the medical staff did all they could to restore him to life, with no success. In fact, one of them, leaving the room with his head down, came to the nurses' station and said to the nurse there, "The man is gone." Immediately, I appealed to the Lord of life in prayer, asking Him to restore Mr. Smith by the mighty power of the "Spirit of life" in Him (Romans 8:2), that great power that raised Lazarus from the dead. No sooner had I said amen than Mr. Smith regained consciousness and asked why so many people were in his room. He stated that he was extremely hungry, and asked if he could have some food.

Another one of the physicians approached the station and

told the nurse to order something from the kitchen, adding, "I have never seen anything like this in all my years."

My prayers had been answered in miraculous ways in that not only was Mr. Smith alive and feeling great, but also the peace of heaven now blessed those present in the intensive care unit. A state of quietness invaded the place. Nurses leisurely stood in the doorways of the glassed-in rooms as their patients actually fell asleep in the peace and comfort previously denied them. As for myself, I could feel the presence of God.

New Leases on Life

For long hours Hilda had been waiting to spend some of her allotted 10 minutes with me. About 10:00 p.m. she came in for the last time that day, before returning to her mother's place for the night. During her stay in the waiting room of the ICU she had become acquainted with Mrs. Smith. The woman had been greatly disturbed over the condition of her husband, who—having given up hope—had actually declared that he wanted to die. Now Mrs. Smith told her of the marvelous—and even miraculous—change in her husband's physical condition, and of the drastic change of attitude he now possessed. Before he had said that he had wanted to die, but now he announced that he wanted to live.

Four days later I had the privilege of meeting the Smiths on the cardiac floor of the hospital. Their joy reflected the peace of God's love. Hilda has been corresponding with the woman, who has informed her that her husband has been in excellent health, and hasn't missed any work since leaving the hospital. He is retiring soon with the prospect of some good years ahead of him.

The day after Mr. Smith's recovery, the doctors discovered that some of their patients in the ICU were well enough to transfer out to other floors of the hospital. The condition of the cardiac patient on my left had changed so much for the better that the hospital moved him immediately, and he was exuberant with joy as he looked forward to a bright future. The elderly man on my right was like a different person. His physician was greatly surprised over the change in his condition, and declared him ready to be transferred the next morning if he continued to improve. It took place on Tuesday morning as anticipated. I was delighted to see my prayers answered before my eyes.

But as for myself, things didn't look good. In fact, at 8:00 a.m. on that Tuesday the cardiologist, answering my questions about my condition, indicated that the possibility of my getting out of the unit alive was extremely slim. Lab tests revealed that a virus had done irreparable damage to my heart.

With my heartbeats so irregular, I simply could not remain alive long in my current state. The doctor suggested one last treatment: to stop my heart with 50 volts of electricity, and restart it with a 200-volt shock. I signed the necessary papers to allow him to proceed. Later that afternoon the cardiologist informed me that the procedure had not helped.

My condition worsened as my lungs filled up with fluid. I realized that I wouldn't last much longer. That evening, although low physically, my mind was alert as I thought back upon almost six decades of living. Scene after scene passed through my mind, and my heart filled with gratitude to God as I saw the care He had exercised over me, even when I had no use for Him. Eventually my memory went back to when I was 7 years of age.

"He is alive! He is still alive!" Edmond, my older brother, shouted after shutting the power off and jumping through a remodeling opening in the floor to the basement below. I had tripped on a block of wood and fallen on a machine strap 14 inches wide. The strap drove a three-foot wheel deriving power from a nine-foot one with the help of a 350-pound tightener spinning on the strap. People had heard my shouts for help way up to the second floor even over the noise of the heavy machinery of the feed mill my father owned in eastern Canada.

If a three-inch steel shaft had not dislodged from its heavy mountings as a violent shock shook the building, I would have instantly perished. But instead the strap fell off the smaller wheel, which in turn caused the tightener to drop off the strap. I had fallen chest down on the strap, which carried me under the larger wheel, then up to the top, where I became wedged against a ceiling beam.

The wheel never slowed down until someone turned the power off. Almost all my clothes were torn off—a heavy winter jacket, a sweater, flannel shirt, and heavy underwear. My left arm was hanging down along the side of the wheel, and friction had worn the top of my hand and fingers down to the bones. For a while the doctor thought he might have to amputate, but I had praying parents who knew by experience the power of prayer in Christ, and all turned out well.

It took three days to repair the damage done to the machinery. According to the millwrights who worked on putting things back in running order, a supernatural force must have caused the damage. They stated that the weight of the tightener alone would have crushed every bone in my body and the machinery wouldn't have slowed down a bit, much less cause that heavy steel shaft to slip out of place. The force that jolted it free, they estimated, had to be equivalent to the impact of an object of one ton.

"Oh that men would praise the Lord for his goodness, and for his wonderful works to the children of men!" (Psalm 107:8).

Yet as I thought over my past, I recalled at age 12 how bitter I became toward God when my mother was lowered in her grave. In my grief I could not adjust to the idea that a good God would allow the suffering of humanity to go on and on, and do nothing to end it. I lost belief in Him and the supernatural. In my late teens I read the works of infidels, then some of Charles Darwin's writings, and to top it all, Thomas Henry Huxley's works convinced me that man was a direct descendant of apes. By the age of 21 I considered myself to be an atheist, having rejected all the Catholic beliefs I ever had, and denied the existence of God. Then unexpectedly I had a most shocking experience with the supernatural. And little did I know that God was watching and caring for me.

It was 1946 in Montreal, Canada, and I met a wartime buddy who had become a member of a society that claimed to communicate with the spirits of the dead. I became involved in their practices, and before long my friend and I were led into a secret society who worshiped super intelligent, beautiful beings whom they referred to as gods. In fact, their worship room contained numerous beautiful paintings of spirits who had materialized, were photographed, then had paintings made of them.

During that time I was working for a Jewish embroidery firm. One of the owners asked me to do him a favor. He had just hired a man who was a Christian but worshiped on Saturday, the seventh day of the week, instead of on Sunday. The boss wanted me to find out what denomination he belonged to. In the process I became deeply interested in what the Bible had to say about the supernatural world of spirits.

A couple days went by; then the spirits informed the high priest of our society that I was studying the Bible and that the gods were furious. Within a few short days the group's leaders offered a $10,000 contract on my life. But the spirits advised that the killing should not be done by anyone outside of the society, and that members should dispose of me by shooting me at a convenient time. The spirits would endow three volunteers with the gift of clairvoyance, enabling them to know where I was at all times. Again the Lord delivered me from an early grave. (A detailed account appears in my book, A *Trip Into the Supernatural.*)

Now, in that hospital bed, although my body was failing, my mind was still clear and sharp. I realized more than ever before the power contained in God's Holy Word, as Psalm 103:10-14 (scriptures memorized years back) went through my mind. "He hath not dealt with us after our sins; nor rewarded us according to our iniquities. For as the heaven is high above the earth, so great is his mercy toward them that fear him. As far as the east is from the west, so far hath he removed our transgressions from us. Like as a father pitieth his children, so the Lord pitieth them that fear him. For he knoweth our frame; he remembereth that we are dust."

Hope, encouragement, and faith sprang into my heart. With joy I recalled that bright sunny Sabbath day of April 1947 when I was baptized and joined the Seventh-day Adventist Church in Montreal, Canada.

In the autumn of that year the Lord greatly enriched my life when on September 20 Hilda and I united in marriage. My young bride was a devout woman who understood the power of intercessory prayer, and who for four decades has been instrumental in securing from on high the divine help that has kept Satan from bringing me to an early grave.

I could remember a number of the freak happenings that could have snuffed out my life had not the Spirit of God miraculously delivered me. For example, one night I was driving near Rushford, New York, on an icy road with snow-banks eight feet high on either side. As I came around a bend I found myself facing a horse standing across that narrow road. Many similar instances passed through my mind.

Now becoming extremely tired, I asked the Lord to give me some rest, and I would converse with Him in prayer at 3:00 a.m. when the nurses would awaken me for my medications.

The Hour of Deliverance

Since 1946 when I had had that unique encounter with demonic spirits, I had experienced moments of fright as I thought about the future. Then the Spirit of God would bless me by leading me to read two portions of Scripture: Revelation 12:11, "And they overcame him by the blood of the Lamb," and Romans 8:38, 39, "I am persuaded, that neither death, nor life, nor angels, nor principalities, nor powers, nor things present, nor things to come, nor height, nor depth, nor any other creature, shall be able to separate us from the love of God, which is in Christ Jesus our Lord."

In that way I learned to fortify myself in the merits of the sacrificial blood of Christ. And in addition, I made it a part of my morning devotions to review the events of that sacrifice by reading Matthew 27:24-54. Such practices have removed all fear of the destroyer, and served to surround me with a spiritual atmosphere of light and peace. So, after taking my medications at 3:00 a.m., I reviewed mentally those verses of Scripture just mentioned. I presented before my great High Priest in the Holy of Holies of the heavenly sanctuary, my personal needs, telling Him that if my pilgrimage through this land of the enemy was coming to an end, it was OK with me, seeing that it is the common lot of humanity to go to the grave sooner or later. But I added, "Lord, if it be pleasing in Thy sight, I would appreciate Your honoring the prayers of the many persons who are praying for my recovery, so that they may see them answered, and their Christian experience strengthened. If so, then bless my damaged heart with the power of the Spirit of life in Thee, that great power that raised Lazarus from the dead, and impart to me strength and energy sufficient to meet the needs and demands of this day."

From experience I had learned that when in faith we take hold of His strength, He will change—wonderfully change—the most hopeless, discouraging outlook, if it is our heavenly Father's will. As I closed my morning devotions an assurance rested upon me that all was well, regardless of what the outcome might be.

I slept soundly till 6:00 a.m. when the lab nurse came to draw some blood. By 7:30 the cardiologist approached my bed with a smile on his face that let me understand that his concern over my condition had lessened. He began by saying that things were looking up, and that a great change for the better had taken place, something he could hardly believe. Pointing to the heart monitor, he said, "The last time I saw you, the monitor was indicating that your heart was beating anywhere between 145 and 185 times per minute. Now it's in the 80s. If your condition holds this good till three o'clock this afternoon, I will have you transferred to the cardiac unit of the hospital."

By 3:00 p.m. my improved condition was holding, and an orderly wheeled me into a lovely room with the sun shining in brightly. Suddenly I realized that my enjoyment of life had grown as never before. Even the dirty city snow somehow awakened in me a new sense of appreciation as I watched the little sparrows bounce around on it.

The Lord had seen me through "the valley of the shadow of death," and I had reached new heights of understanding about the power of intercessory prayer. And though I had almost passed through the portal of the tomb, I now valued the experience, realizing that the Lord of glory had been at my side through the presence of His Spirit in a way that I had never known before.

Almost a week to the hour that I had been admitted to the

emergency room, I walked out of the hospital on my own two feet. Those feet may not have moved very fast, but they did carry me again to the world outside, and that was wonderful.

2

Standing in Holy Time

It was early in my Christian experience—and providential in a way—that I found myself needing a special blessing from the Spirit of God.

One Wednesday evening in October, 1947, exactly a year after I began studying God's Holy Word, I went to a prayer meeting in our SDA French-speaking church in Montreal, Canada. Afterward the pastor asked if I could do him a favor. Part of his duties consisted of spending every third weekend with the members of the French-speaking church in Quebec City. He had been giving Bible studies to a Mr. and Mrs. Gauvin, a sincere couple who loved the Lord with all their hearts.

Jehovah's Witnesses also began studying the Bible with them. After a time the Gauvins became confused and distressed. Not only had they made drastic changes in their lives in giving up the rituals and beliefs of the Roman Catholic Church, but now they encountered a crisis that they could not resolve.

Mr. Gauvin told our pastor that after each Bible study with him, they felt that the Adventists had the truth about the ideal way of serving God. Then the Witnesses would come along and after their session with them, the couple would feel that the latter were right. The Gauvins came to the point where they could take no more of such a yo-yo type of existence.

Then they decided how they would solve the problem

forever—have both an SDA minister and a Jehovah's Witness one face-to-face in a discussion. Would our pastor be willing to participate in such a debate? The Witnesses had agreed to it and were looking forward to what they felt would be the greatest event of the year, and a major victory to the honor of Jehovah. Our pastor agreed to a meeting on a date to be set later.

On that particular Wednesday morning our minister received a call from Mr. Gauvin that the debate would take place on the coming Saturday evening at 8:00 p.m. He would face the top leader of the Witnesses, the person in charge of their French missions in all of Canada. Gauvin added that the man was a former Catholic priest holding a Doctor of Divinity degree.

"So, Brother Morneau, would you do me a favor?" my pastor now asked. "Would you take my place? I have to attend meetings starting on Sunday morning at the Ontario-Quebec Conference session in Oshawa, Ontario. The president tells me that I cannot miss them."

"What about the first elder?" I protested.

"I have already talked to him, and he cannot help since an important family event will take him away this weekend." My pastor assured me that I was well prepared for the task because I had memorized all the important verses of Scripture that would clearly set forth the sacredness of the Bible Sabbath, and besides, the Lord would surely be with me.

Glancing at my young bride, I asked, "What do you think of this?" She stated that she felt confident that God would be with me, and besides, it could turn out to be a valuable experience, "one that I would look back upon with delight."

"Pastor," I said, "I will go, but with a deep sense of helplessness. Like Moses I say, 'Who am I, that I should go unto Pharaoh?' "

Early Friday morning Hilda and I took the train for Quebec City. The trip was enjoyable, as it was a beautiful, cool, crisp day, and all of nature seemed to speak silently to one's heart that the great Monarch of the galaxies was looking kindly over our planet.

The Gauvins had informed us that they would be delighted to have us stay with them for the weekend, and would pick us up at the train station. The meeting would take place in the residence of one of the Witnesses, and only a few people were supposed to be there, mostly individuals that had been taking Bible studies with them. Mrs. Gauvin declined to attend after one of the Witnesses informed her over the phone that it was going to be a vigorous, unyielding contention. Hilda decided to stay at home with her.

Arriving on time, Mr. Gauvin and I found to our surprise a great number of people present. The large living room and dining room were packed tight. The Jehovah's Witness leader was unhappy over the fact that the Adventist minister could not make it. He felt slighted, and stated that he had never debated a neophyte before. Twenty minutes of his time should settle the matter in question once and for all, proving without a question of a doubt that Jehovah's Witnesses have the truth. The 20 minutes turned out to be two and a half hours in length.

The man's arguments and reasoning were hard to follow, as he kept going around in circles with his theology. Whenever I confronted him with proof from the Bible, he would quickly make a U-turn and circle in the opposite direction. It was a bit like trying to get a rabbit out of one's fenced garden. As soon as you corner the little creature, he jumps in an unexpected direction, and you just can't catch him.

For instance, the man claimed that Jesus did not rise from the grave in bodily form, but in a spiritual body—a spirit form. In response I read Luke 24:36-43 that tells how Jesus appeared before His disciples on the Resurrection evening. "Jesus himself stood in the midst of them, and saith unto them, Peace be unto you. But they were terrified and affrighted, and supposed that they had seen a spirit. And he said unto them, Why are ye troubled? and why do thoughts arise in your hearts? Behold my hands and my feet, that it is I myself: handle me, and see; for a spirit hath not flesh and bones, as ye see me have."

The Jehovah's Witness stated that he was well aware of those scriptures, but that one could not take them at face value. Then he proceeded by using bits of Scripture here and there, taken out of context, to place a totally different light on the subject.

We covered many topics, and in all the Spirit of God fortified my thinking with reasoning backed up by the Word of God. At one point Mr. Gauvin wanted to hear us discuss the matter of the seventh-day Sabbath so that he could make an intelligent decision.

As expected, the Witness leader quickly stated that "the Jewish Sabbaths had been nailed to the cross of Christ, and done away with. It forever freed men of demands placed upon the Jews as they came out of slavery, a necessary restraint at the time, intended to break their stubborn and unruly behavior. It was a day used to teach them about God. But now we are free in Christ, and can put the seventh day of the week to better use."

I replied that God never meant that man should consider the seventh-day Sabbath as a Jewish institution. In fact, the Creator declared its true intent and purpose in no uncertain words at the end of the Creation week. "And on the seventh day God ended his work which he had made; and he rested on the seventh day from all his work which He had made. And God blessed the seventh day, and sanctified it: because that in it he had rested from all his work which God created and made" (Genesis 2:2, 3).

Clearly God intended that the biblical Sabbath should stand forever as a memorial of His capacity not only to create, but also to sustain His creation for ages to come. And its purpose was to bring a special blessing to all those who observed that day in a devotional frame of mind.

I also read the fourth commandment with great care, placing the proper emphasis at the right places, while at the same time praying that the Spirit of God would indelibly write those sacred words on everyone's mind.

It was not possible to give a regular Bible study on the Sabbath, because the man relentlessly contested everything I said. If it had not been for Mr. Gauvin, I would have excused myself and left. But I determined by God's grace to tough it out.

The Jehovah's Witness leader kept harping that Christ had nailed to His cross the handwriting of ordinances, taking it out of the way of the Christian. For once I could agree with him, and told him so.

I explained that God had used those institutions to teach the children of Israel about the infinite sacrifice that the Lord of glory would accomplish on Calvary. When Christ died on the cross, they lost their purpose.

Then I read Deuteronomy 31:24-26. "And it came to pass, when Moses had made an end of writing the words of this law in a book, until they were finished, that Moses commanded the Levites, which bare the ark of the covenant of the Lord, saying, Take this book of the law, and put it in the side of the ark of the covenant of the Lord your God, that it may be there for a witness against thee."

Then I established the fact that God had written the moral law—which included the Bible Sabbath—with His own finger on two tables of stone. The Israelites deposited them inside the ark of the covenant, while they placed the ordinances written by Moses on the outside between the ark and a retaining board. Most of those present showed great surprise at grasping the distinction.

My next approach was to establish in their minds the solemnity—and vast difference—that exists in God's sight between that which He declares to be holy, and that which is common and ordinary.

First I recounted the sad experience of Nadab and Abihu, who lost their lives while officiating in the sanctuary. They had never learned to differentiate between the holy and the unholy, and went about doing their own thing. "And Nadab and Abihu, the sons of Aaron, took either of them his censer, and put fire therein, and put incense thereon, and offered strange fire before the Lord, which he commanded them not. And there went out fire from the Lord, and devoured them, and they died before the Lord" (Leviticus 10:1, 2).

It was a sad and shocking experience the parents of those young adults had to go through in order for the Lord to teach the children of Israel the distinction between holy and unholy. Verse 10 of the same chapter tells us that God informed Aaron of the lesson that His people should learn from the tragedy: "That ye may put difference between holy and unholy, and unclean and clean."

Then I asked, "Shouldn't we pay close attention to God's commandment to remember the Sabbath day to keep it holy?" A number of them replied that they now saw that the matter deserved consideration. But the Jehovah's Witness pastor wasn't impressed. In fact, he stated that God in Old Testament times was not always so demanding. "Take, for instance," he said, "our first parents. When Adam was unable to father female offspring, one of the boys had to have sexual relations with his mother in order to begin populating the earth."

Naturally I couldn't believe my ears. And I became aware that while the man had acquired vast amounts of knowledge in many fields, he clearly did not know much about the Word of God. He was shocked when I had him turn to Genesis 5:4 and read, "And the days of Adam after he had begotten Seth were eight hundred years: and he begat sons and daughters." Then he said, "This shows that one can always learn something new regardless of how old he is."

Unfortunately he started to go around in circles again. He asked for about 10 minutes to illustrate how the Bible does not always mean what it says. I gave him the go-ahead, as I needed a little time myself to petition God to touch the hearts of the group in a way that they had never experienced before—especially Mr. Gauvin.

As I began to pray I tuned out what the man was saying. I didn't care what he was speaking about. Instead I petitioned, "Our Father in heaven, Thou great Monarch of the galaxies, I appeal to Thee at this time through the merits of the precious blood of Christ Jesus the Lord of glory, shed on Calvary for the salvation of fallen humanity. Father, I realize that I am getting nowhere with what I have been saying up to this point. I need help, and I need it badly. People here may well be making decisions this evening that will determine whether they will find themselves living in the earth made new. Oh, that I had the tongue of an angel! But Father, You have something far better to offer: the mighty power of the third person of the Godhead. The Spirit of life, through whom alone we can resist and overcome sin and have our stony hearts changed and filled with Thine own love. Lord, may the Holy Spirit do a little housecleaning right now. Rebuke the power of Satan and his angels, then surround all of us here with a divine atmosphere of light and peace, so that each one will be able to make intelligent decisions this evening. Thank You again, Lord, for hearing and answering my prayers."

Instantly a thought entered my mind: talk to them about distrust of God and the unbelief that fills the human heart, and how it will destroy vast numbers of people for eternity. "That's it, Lord, that's it. Thank You, precious Father, Thank you."

Being a young convert, I had been studying the Word of God diligently and had just finished reading the Old Testament along with *Patriarchs and Prophets* and *Prophets and Kings*. One thing from my reading that had impressed me above everything else was the fact that the fallen human heart by nature seethes with distrust of God and unbelief. We cannot escape it unless God's Holy Spirit works a daily miracle of redemption in us.

As soon as the Jehovah's Witness leader had wound down and I had a chance to talk again, I said, "Friends, the reason we find ourselves here this evening is because we love the Lord Jesus who gave His life for us on Calvary, and we want to serve Him with our whole heart. But the way to do it is at times not really clear in our minds, and we find an inner turmoil going on inside us. We may even become utterly confused. It may interest you to hear that millions of individuals before you have had the very same experience."

Realizing that I had a captive audience, I continued, "You see, we have in our fallen nature a powerful element that constantly seeks to separate us from our Creator, and will surely destroy us unless God's Holy Spirit breaks that distrust and unbelief. Without that help, we are sunk." Never before had they listened so attentively.

"To verify what I am saying, all we have to do is to check what the Bible tells us about those who will miss out on eternal life. We read of Cain, who killed his brother because Abel's trust was a constant rebuke to him. Think of the multitudes of antediluvians who perished in the Flood. Or of the descendants of Noah whose distrust and unbelief led them to build the Tower of Babel. By the time God called Abraham out of Ur of the Chaldees, such distrust and unbelief had spread throughout the human race. Remember the children of Israel who for 40 years wandered in the wilderness because their unbelief shut them out from the Promised Land."

I could tell by their expressions that the Spirit of God was moving with power. "Friends, distrust of God and unbelief has often blocked God's blessings. The Bible says of Jesus, 'He did not many mighty works there because of their unbelief' (Matthew 13:58).

"Think of it—people depriving themselves of the blessings of God because of their unbelief. That is sad, sad, sad." For about five to seven seconds the place was so quiet that you could have heard a pin drop. I waited to see which way the Spirit of God would lead.

"What must we do to be helped here?" Mr. Gauvin asked, breaking the silence.

"All I can tell you is what I have personally experienced, and how it has blessed my life. In Ephesians 2:8 we read: 'By grace are ye saved through faith.' And friends, to my estimation, grace is the power of the Holy Spirit in action. So every morning I pray, "Our Father in heaven, I plead the merits of the precious blood of Christ shed on Calvary as the reason that I should receive help in the warfare against evil. By the mighty power of Your Holy Spirit working in my behalf, please save me this day from self, from sin, from the world, and from the power of the fallen angels. Save me from self, by removing from my heart distrust and unbelief, and replace it with a living faith in Thee, so that I can take Thee at Thy word. Thank You, Lord, for Your grace and Your love."

I explained how such prayer had brought me peace, contentment, and wisdom. "I think it's a wise person who takes God at His word. If you recall, as Moses approached the burning bush, the Lord said, 'Draw not nigh hither: put off thy shoes from off thy feet, for the place whereon thou standest is holy ground" (Exodus 3:5). Had Moses distrusted and disbelieved God, he would have said, 'Lord I don't see any difference in this soil. Are You sure that this sand right here is

27

holy ground?' But Moses took God at His word, as it was his way of life.

"Folks, we can have a burning bush experience in the way Moses did, by remembering the seventh-day Sabbath to keep it holy. You and I may not stand on holy ground, but we can stand in holy time, by taking God at His word, and respect the sacredness of His holy Sabbath day."

"Your experience, Mr. Morneau, is debatable," the Jehovah's Witness interrupted.

Instantly Mr. Gauvin stood, and raising his hands in a gesture to stop him, said, "Pastor, that will not be necessary. What Brother Morneau has told us, I have already experienced, right here, right now. I have prayed his prayer along with him. The Spirit of God has opened my understanding, and I have made up my mind. From this day on my family and I will serve God in the way He wants us to. We will be Seventh-day Adventists, for they have the truth for these times."

When I heard those words, my heart thrilled with a joy born of heaven. What a fantastic victory for Christ God's Holy Spirit had achieved in that place.

Yes, my wife had been right when she said that the experience could turn out to be one that I would look back upon with great delight.

A few months later Mr. and Mrs. Gauvin and their children moved to Montreal, in order for the youngsters to attend church school. And for a period of six years before we came to the States the Gauvins were some of our best friends.

How wonderful it is that our God makes us avenues for His Spirit to bless others. And statements like the following have helped me to expect great things from God: "To us today, as verily as to the first disciples, the promise of the Spirit belongs. . . . At this very hour His Spirit and His grace are for all who need them and will take Him at His word" (*Testimonies*, vol. 8, p. 20).

CHAPTER
3

Growing in Grace
and Knowledge of God

Before I consider the important factors that activate the power of intercessory prayer, I feel it's important to relate first a number of experiences that God used to prepare me so that He could then bless others through my intercessions. They helped me to see both the importance and power of intercessory prayer.

The apostle Peter in his Second Epistle to the Christians of his day lost no time in wishing them the very best in their Christian walk and calling their attention to the fact that divine blessings could actually increase in their lives if only they acquired a better understanding of our heavenly Father and Jesus our Lord. "Grace and peace be multiplied unto you through the knowledge of God, and of Jesus our Lord, according as his divine power hath given unto us all things that pertain unto life and godliness" (2 Peter 1:2, 3).

A similar passage in the writings of Ellen G. White has done more for my Christian experience than I could ever have imagined possible. On the last page of *The Great Controversy*, she wrote, "And the years of eternity, as they roll, will bring richer and still more glorious revelations of God and of Christ. As knowledge is progressive, so will love, reverence, and happiness increase. The more men learn of God, the greater will be their admiration of His character" (p. 678).

The more I thought upon those words, the more excited I became about being in the earth made new. And I said to myself, Why wait to be immortalized to enjoy that kind of an experience? Why not enjoy it now? After memorizing those lines so that they would become meaningful to me, I began asking the Lord on a daily basis to impart to me the grace needed in my life to make the above become reality here and now. Here is one of many experiences that did it for me.

It happened in the wintertime, January to be exact. For a number of days I had been studying the biblical concept of faith. While Scripture speaks of vast numbers of people having had their lives ruled by distrust of God and unbelief, it also reveals how certain persons acquired a living faith by developing an unfaltering trust in our heavenly Father, and in the power of His Holy Spirit.

An Ellen White statement had also encouraged me: "Faith is inspired by the Holy Spirit, and it will flourish only as it is cherished" (Great Controversy, p. 527). I decided to keep thanking the Lord for all the many times in my life when His Spirit had given me faith, and asked Him to increase it.

That particular morning in my devotions I read the experience of Philip in Acts 8, where an angel told him to go south of Jerusalem on the road to Gaza. There he saw the treasurer of Candace, queen of Ethiopia, sitting in his chariot reading a scroll of Isaiah. Then the Spirit of God said to Philip, "Go near, and join thyself to this chariot."

As a result, a baptism took place, and the Bible says that "when they were come out of the water, the Spirit of the Lord caught away Philip." And he found himself at Azotus, a little town about 20 miles from where he had left the Ethiopian eunuch.

Reading the story, I said to myself, *What exciting times those days were when the Spirit of God was so close to people.* And through the rest of that day I meditated on the biblical story.

In those days I was a salesman, and that evening I had a 9:00 p.m. appointment with a building contractor living on a rural road about four miles west of Castile, New York. Our home was in Curriers, about seven miles north of Arcade. To avoid a route that would have forced me to go east in a roundabout way, I had gotten instructions to go cross-country on some county roads that would supposedly save me a lot of travel time. Unfortunately, it didn't. I got lost three times because of the constant crossroads, and I made wrong turns. It meant stopping and asking directions at farms, and I arrived almost an hour late.

On my way there I realized that my gas gauge had dropped rather low, but reasoned that the best thing to do was to fill the tank in Castile afterward. We got involved talking business, and time flew by. When I had finished writing up an order and was ready to leave, my watch indicated almost midnight. By then the thought of getting gasoline had left me. The contractor, desiring to save me going into Castile in order to take Route 39, a state road that would carry me west into Arcade and home, suggested that I drive three miles west from his residence, then take a left that would get me directly onto Route 39.

I was reluctant to go that way, but he said I couldn't make a wrong turn because of a huge landmark at that intersection. As I stepped out on the porch, the cold chilled me instantly. He looked at his thermometer, which read five degrees below zero.

"I hope you have a good battery," he said.

"Yes, sir. One of the best for winter driving." Waving goodbye, I left. Because of the bitter cold, it took longer than usual to get heat into the car, and it absorbed all my attention. I had traveled about five miles when all of a sudden the engine began to lose power. A glance at the gas gauge told me the tank was empty. Terror struck my mind as I realized that the last farm I had passed was more than a mile away, and no more were in sight.

Like a flash I saw myself in a hospital bed with my toes cut off. You see, when I was 17 years of age, I froze all my toes one morning in northern Quebec when the temperature had gone down to 42 below. I spent five months in the hospital. The flesh turned black and actually fell off my toes. Afterward I had a number of operations, skin grafts, etc. And the day of my discharge the surgeon who had worked on my feet sat me down and stated that I should no longer live in that part of the world. He believed that my feet would quickly freeze if exposed to the cold, and that the only thing that could be done then would be to amputate.

Now in a burst of fear I cried out, "Dear Jesus, please help." Many times before when certain destruction stared me in the face, I had made that call for help, and Jesus had never failed me. Immediately a great calm came over me. But the car was still slowing down.

"Forgive me for being so panicky, seeing that You have never failed me," I thought. "O Lord, I know that the Spirit of God that transported Philip 20 miles so long ago can get me and this car over those hills into Curriers if He so chooses. Dear Jesus, may the Spirit of God that controls the atoms please fuel this car so it will take me home without stopping. Thank You, Lord, for Your help."

It was almost as if something hit the back of my automobile, and it shot forward; then the motor started to accelerate and hummed like never before. The speedometer climbed and when it reached the speed limit I had to release my foot from the pedal, as the vehicle kept dashing ahead. Eagle Hill—which I had never climbed without the transmission shifting down—I now sped up in high gear. Jubilantly I praised the Lord for His miracle-working power.

I began quoting verses of Scripture, such as Psalm 107:1, 2, and 8. "O give thanks unto the Lord, for he is good: for his mercy endureth for ever. Let the redeemed of the Lord say so, whom he hath redeemed from the hand of the enemy." "Oh that men would praise the Lord for his goodness, and for his wonderful works to the children of men."

Praising the Lord with my whole heart and at the same time crying for joy, I felt the words of Psalm 105:1-5 had never sounded so wonderful. "O give thanks unto the Lord; call upon his name: make known his deeds among the people. Sing unto him, sing Psalms unto him: Talk ye of all his wonderous works. Glory ye in his holy name: let the heart of them rejoice that seek the Lord. Seek the Lord and his strength: seek his face evermore. Remember his marvellous works that he hath done; his wonders, and the judgments of his mouth."

After I pulled into the driveway, up a small grade, and past the side entrance of our house, the car stopped. It did not reach the garage. Turning the ignition off, I ran into the house, surprised to see the lights on in the kitchen.

About 11:45 p.m. Hilda had awakened, and realizing that I was not home yet, got on her knees and prayed for God's loving care over me. As I entered, she knew that something great and wonderful had happened. "You look excited. What's the good news?"

I recounted how the Spirit of God had brought me home 27 miles without any gas in the tank. We had a praise session to the Lord that probably lasted an hour, then went to bed but could not sleep most of the night, as we kept talking about my experience.

In the morning I tried to start the car, but it would not. We had to fetch gasoline from the neighbor's farm to get it going.

Facing Death and No Time to Pray

Nothing prepares a person for sincere heartfelt prayer as the threat of death. And I have found by experience that nothing calms fear as well as memorizing verses of Scripture that tell of God's deliverance in ages past. During times of need the Spirit of God fortifies the mind with the power inherent in the Word of God. In the not-far-distant future God's commandment-keeping people will go through some mind-shattering experiences as the forces of darkness will redouble their efforts to shake and destroy all those that are not anchored on the Rock of Ages.

I have had experiences that would have driven me crazy were it not that I had fortified my mind in the Word of God, and trusted the Lord to carry me through whatever He would allow to come my way. And let me tell you that once you have gone through the fire (so to speak) and the Spirit of God has brought you through safely, you are a different person. You feel so much closer to God.

In late March, about two months after the previous incident, we had a lot of snow in the western New York area. In Wyoming County around the Arcade-Rushford area, snowplows had piled up mounds in some places as high as 10 feet. But the rigor of winter was beginning to abate, the sun was gaining strength, and the days were getting longer.

One particular evening while I traveled home I occupied my time memorizing 2 Chronicles 16:9: "The eyes of the Lord run to and fro throughout the whole earth, to shew himself strong in the behalf of them whose heart is perfect toward Him." By then I neared Rushford, driving at a reasonable rate of speed and slowing down before each turn in the road, as it was impossible to see if any vehicles were coming around the corner.

Suddenly I came upon a stretch of road that was quite slippery, as some of the snow had thawed during the day, then refroze when the sun went down, leaving large patches of ice. It was impossible to brake lest I lose control of the car. Touching neither brake or accelerator, I let the car roll into the curve with the hope that nothing approached from the opposite direction.

As I rounded the corner I saw a large horse standing in the middle of the road. There was no way to avoid hitting it. My hands froze on the stirring wheel, and all I could say in a call for help was "Dear Jesus." Instantly some force, which I believe to be the Spirit of God, since I felt the exact same presence that night two months before, wrestled the steering wheel out of my hands and directed the car toward the front legs of the horse. Just a moment before impact the animal reared up on its hind legs, and I slumped in my seat to avoid the hoofs hitting me in the face through the windshield.

They cleared the car probably by one or two inches. A short distance down the road I managed to bring the car to a stop and give my pounding heart a couple minutes to recover and at the same time send forth a prayer of thanks.

Realizing the danger to other motorists, I drove to the first house down the road to see if the horse belonged there. When I explained what had happened, the man stated that the animal belonged to a neighbor and was kept indoors during the winter months. Picking up the phone, he contacted the owner, who declared that his horse had been in its stall a half hour ago when he had completed his evening chores. However, he would check and call right back.

A few minutes later the message came that in some mysterious way the horse had gotten out. The stall door was wide open, the barn door was ajar, and the animal was gone.

Neither man could figure out how it could have taken place. Nobody could have reached the barn without someone seeing him, since the driveway faced a large picture window in the kitchen where the family had been at the time. "It's strange, strange," they said.

My wife and I had another praise session to our heavenly Father. On the following Sabbath I recounted the experience to my Sabbath school class, and the people rejoiced with me. Death had stared me in the face, but the eyes of the Lord had been upon me, and His Spirit brought deliverance. That incident helped me to grow in knowledge of God.

Lamentations 3:22-26 contains special words of hope and assurance of God's loving care over those who place their lives in His protection. "It is of the Lord's mercies that we are not consumed, because his compassions fail not. They are new every morning; great is thy faithfulness. The Lord is my portion, saith my soul; therefore will I hope in him. The Lord is good unto them that wait for him, to the soul that seeketh him. It is good that a man should both hope and quietly wait for the salvation of the Lord."

Many times over the years my heart has lifted up to God in thanksgiving whenever the Spirit of God brought me out of impossible situations.

For almost 20 years I worked in telephone directory advertising sales (yellow pages) for both the Bell and Continental telephone systems in Ohio, New York, and Pennsylvania. For the last five of those years, I was division sales manager for the Mast Advertising and Publishing firm of Overland Park, Kansas, publishers of directories for Continental Telephone and other independent telephone companies. I had charge of directory people in the Northeast Division, covering an area of eight states.

Yearly I traveled anywhere between 25,000 and 45,000 miles. I was on the road in rainstorms, snowstorms, dense fog, and other unfavorable conditions. Frequently I saw cars hurtling at me that were undoubtedly driven by drunks or individuals with their minds spaced out on drugs.

To be crushed in a car on a highway is something that doesn't attract much media attention in this day and age, but to be smashed in a car in a Sears parking lot could get front-page attention.

In December 1971 I was working on the Watertown, New York, telephone directory. For a few nights it had been exceedingly cold for that time of the year, and I wanted to assure myself that my battery would not fail me one morning, so I proceeded to the Sears auto department to have it checked.

It was a busy morning in the service department, undoubtedly brought about by the cold spell that had taken many by surprise. Being unable to bring the car indoors (the bays were filled), the service manager brought a tester out to the car, performed the necessary checks, and announced that the battery would carry me through another winter without any problems.

Meanwhile a large tractor-trailer loaded with 27 tons of cargo had parked sideways behind my car while the driver went inside the store to get unloading instructions. My car faced the building, making it impossible to get away. At the time I was driving a small Saab. The manager suggested that I back up under the body of the huge trailer, as there was sufficient room to do so. He would guide me in the maneuver.

The truck motor was turned off and the brakes set, or otherwise it would have rolled down the hill, since the parking lot was on a steep incline.

Slowly I backed under the trailer while the service manager directed me. When I had all of the car under the trailer except the motor, suddenly I felt that same feeling of urgency that I had experienced in previous emergencies. I remember bringing the gearshift out of reverse position; then what seemed to be a powerful and sudden push propelled the car forward. If I had not had my foot on the brake I would have hit the building. Even with that lunge forward, the vehicle did not get completely out of the path of the truck that suddenly shot backward, hitting the rear bumper and knocking the taillight off the fender. The blow shoved the back part of the car sideways about three feet.

The people who had been watching me back up under the trailer ran to the car to see if I was all right. Although shaken some, I was not hurt. They kept repeating, "Are you all right? Man, are you ever fortunate. You were almost killed. How did you get that car forward so quickly? How did you know that the truck was going to roll? How were you able to stop the car from going into the brick wall?" One elderly woman declared, "Your angel saved your life. God must certainly love you a lot." A man said, "Fellow, you were almost crushed flat into that car. Do you realize that?"

The tractor-trailer damaged several cars, jackknifed, then stopped as it demolished the back half of a large Chrysler. The driver of the rig appeared on the scene in time to see his vehicle crash into the last car. Unable to believe his eyes, he emphatically declared that he had the truck in forward gear and that the emergency brake was on.

The owner of the Chrysler was furious. He and his wife had gotten out of the car just a few seconds before the accident and were walking up to the store; they had to run out of the way to avoid being hit. He began accusing the driver of being many unflattering things, including being an idiot for leaving a truck standing without the brakes secured properly. Determined to check them there and then, he started for the cab, but the driver refused to let anyone enter it and stayed out of it himself until the Watertown police could get there and make an accident report.

A great number of people gathered quickly, everyone curious to know what had taken place. They were amazed that I had esc.aped certain death. When the police arrived they tried to disperse the crowd and clear the way so that traffic could move, but the people didn't want to leave.

One of the officers climbed into the cab of the truck to examine the controls. He stated to his partner that the ignition was off and the gear shift was in neutral, and the light on the dashboard indicated that the brakes were on. Naturally he couldn't figure out what had happened that would have allowed the truck to roll as it did.

When he prepared his report I was the first one he interviewed. At the close, he said, "Mr. Morneau, you are a very lucky person in the fact that you are alive at this moment. A second longer under that trailer, and you would not be here making an accident report. Instead you would have made the front page of the evening paper, and I can imagine how that would read."

As I drove away, the words "It is of the Lord's mercies that we are not consumed, because his compassions fail not. They are new every morning" went through my mind.

4

Jesus' Intensive Care Unit

As I studied the power and impact of intercessory prayer in the Bible and the writings of Ellen White, I concluded that one needs to be fitted in a special way to conduct a successful prayer ministry.

The most important thing we must receive is a mind like that of Christ. "Let this mind be in you, which was also in Christ Jesus" (Philippians 2:5), Paul said. When Eutychus "fell down from the third loft, and was taken up dead," he could say, "Trouble not yourselves; for his life is in him" (Acts 20:9, 10). He had seen his silent prayers answered before his eyes so many times that he knew without a doubt that God had heard the cry of his heart as he ran downstairs to the youth.

I can imagine him saying, "Dear Jesus, Thou art Lord of the impossible. Please turn this misfortune around so that Thy people will exalt Thy great name in a praise session that will continue the rest of their lives as they think back upon this event. Thank You, Lord, for Your love and Your grace."

So I began to pray for the Holy Spirit to impart the mind of Christ to me. But after a while the Spirit of God led me to understand that I didn't really know what I was asking for, and that God cannot really answer us when we stay on the level of generalities.

From that time on my prayers took on a whole new meaning. No longer did I use vague expressions, such as "Lord, please bless this person." Instead I asked that God would bless a person in a specific way, so that I would then be able to see that He was answering my prayers as the very things I had asked for took place before my eyes. In other words, I was learning to pray meaningful prayers, and to understand that we cannot rush through them. Unhurried, meaningful prayer is time consuming and at first unappealing to the human mind, but I discovered that it produces great results.

As I continued praying to receive the mind of Christ, it became clear that a mind like His would mean that I would think as He thinks and feel as He feels about life on our fallen planet until I in turn began to act as He would if He were in my place. In other words, I would find myself having a lifestyle patterned after His own righteous mind.

I had read in Ellen White's writings that the early disciples had hoped and prayed for a similar experience to crown their own lives while they waited for the fulfillment of the promise of the Spirit.

"As they meditated upon His pure holy life they felt that no toil would be too hard, no sacrifice too great, if only they could bear witness in their lives to the loveliness of Christ's character" (The Acts of the Apostles, p. 36).

While my reasoning was to a large extent correct, I did not really understand the vastness of the blessings that await us through the character of Christ. I had just touched upon only a very small part of what constitutes the mind of Christ. As I read further in Scripture and Mrs. White, my understanding grew. For instance, Mrs. White wrote about our Saviour, "Not for Himself, but for others, He lived and thought and prayed. . . . Daily He received a fresh baptism of the Holy Spirit" (Christ's Object Lessons, p. 139). I concluded that I could not expect to operate successfully in a world of sin with less grace than what Jesus had prayed for and received during His life on earth.

Now I added to my daily petitions to God a request for a fresh baptism of the Holy Spirit. I asked that the Spirit of God would enable me to obtain a greater knowledge of my Lord and Saviour, and the power of His resurrection, something that the apostle Paul had craved for (Philippians 3:10). And to my great amazement, things began to take place in my life that I had not expected and would never have thought possible.

During the middle 1960s, while I worked on the Hudson, Ohio, telephone directory, God especially blessed my Christian experience and began to make of me ᵔ channel for "the outflowing of the highest influence in the universe" (*Testimonies* vol. 8, p. 22). A few months previous I had changed my line of work by going into telephone directory advertising sales. After nearly a month at the training school in Dayton, Ohio, the company assigned me to work on small telephone directories in New York state to gain experience. Soon they put me on larger projects, and before long they appointed me to the Hudson, Ohio, telephone directory, a geographical area covered by the Mid-Continent telephone system.

In addition to business accounts assigned to me in the local Hudson telephone area, I had to contact business firms located in the cities of Akron, Kent, and Ravenna. The work was interesting, but at the same time rather demanding. It challenged one's creativity to make up ads that would meet each firm's needs. If the ads you made did not bring in customers, the next year the owner would cancel them.

Each evening we would prepare ads designed to be both appealing and informative. It took six individuals three weeks to make up the Hudson directory, while in the case of the Buffalo, New York, telephone book 43 persons spent six months covering that market area.

Time was at a premium in that one had to handle a certain number of accounts each day in order to close the directory on time. Visiting the business in person could be time-consuming if advertisers carried ads at many classifications and had acquired different product lines. That required a change of copy to put in the new information and to delete what was no longer needed.

One factor that had a lot to do with one's success was finding the business owners in their establishments. If they were out, it meant calling back later, which consumed valuable time and kept you from seeing some of your other customers. All one needed to get into a crisis situation was to have the misfortune of having many of the owners out two or three days in a row. Besides, when you get pressed for time, tension mounts, and it's hard to operate effectively.

Because of the fact that businesspeople face great pressure, if the yellow pages representative can't maintain a cheerful, pleasant, and diplomatic attitude, he may lose advertising revenue or the contract altogether. Early in the game I learned that I needed to pray on the run in order to succeed. I quickly understood that I needed special blessings from God to keep from burning out under pressure.

In fact, I would not have gone into that line of work were it not that I believed firmly in the formula for success that the Lord gave Joshua when he took responsibility for leading the children of Israel. "As I was with Moses, so I will be with thee. ... Only be thou strong and very courageous, that thou mayest observe to do according to all the law, which Moses my servant commanded thee: turn not from it to the right hand or to the left, that thou mayest prosper whithersoever thou goest. This book of the law shall not depart out of thy mouth; but thou shalt meditate therein day and night, that thou mayest observe to do according to all that is written therein: for then thou shalt make thy way prosperous, and then thou shalt have good success" (Joshua 1:5-8).

As one of God's commandment-observing people, I felt that the Lord would be with me in a similar manner.

During my work on the Hudson, Ohio, telephone directory the statement from *Christ's Object Lessons* kept going through my mind: "Not for Himself, but for others, He lived and thought and prayed. . . . Daily He received a fresh baptism of the Holy Spirit." As I prayed for a similar power to enter my life, a change began to take place in the way I looked at, and felt about, the lives of others.

One morning I called on an automobile body repairing and painting shop. As I reviewed the copy in his display ad, the owner stated that he needed a few days to make up his mind, as he was contemplating closing the business (if he did, he would cancel his ad). I asked why he would do a thing like that, when he had what seemed to be a very progressive operation.

"I might as well tell you about my problem. Would you please close the office door?"

As I sat down again, he said, "I don't know why I am telling you this, when I have told no one else. I have a bad situation at home that is getting worse by the day. My wife and I are not getting along anymore, and I have come to the point that I feel like closing this shop, moving to California with my 16-year-old son, and filing for divorce. That's why it's so difficult for me to make a final decision about my advertising."

Considering the pressure of my schedule and the training I had received, the right thing for me to have done in such a case would have been to cancel the man's advertising (I would need his signature to cancel) and to explain that I could put it back in if he called the telephone business office before the date that the book went to the printers. That would have saved me the trouble of coming back, which would have enabled me to use my time selling advertising to other business firms.

But I didn't do that, because I kept hearing those words, "Not for Himself, but for others, He lived and thought and prayed." I felt strongly that I should have the man unload his burden while I silently prayed for him. Then I asked, "Do you mind telling me how things got so bad?"

"It began about three years ago," he said, "shortly after we moved into our beautiful new house. My wife began to place silly demands upon me. She complained that I was not giving her enough of my time, and that I loved my business more than her. I agreed that I did spend a lot of time managing the business—to serve the public is time-consuming. And I tried to explain that in order to acquire all the things she had asked for, I had to work long hours and there was no getting around that fact. But somehow she could not understand that, and kept nagging and accusing me of being hard-hearted. The time came when she got enraged to the point of throwing dishes on the floor."

"Have you thought of getting professional counseling on the matter?"

"Yes, we went that route last year. It helped for a while, but her anger kept coming back. I tell you, she is not the same person I have known for so many years. She can be real sweet, then for no reason at all her personality changes, and she becomes mean and ugly. One thing I do know for sure is that I cannot continue living like this."

I would have liked to talk to him about God, but I could not because in training school the instructors had told us in no uncertain words that it was against company policy to talk politics or religion with yellow pages customers, and that company time is strictly for conducting business.

Instead I suggested that I would return in two weeks to give him a chance to decide about his yellow pages ad. He felt good about that, and as I left his place of business, I mentioned that I would remember him and his wife in my prayers. The man thanked me for my interest in his problem.

As I was driving to my next call, thinking about his difficulties, I felt a deep concern for the couple's well-being, something I had never experienced before toward complete strangers. Then the Spirit of God brought back something I had memorized long before. "The Son of God, looking upon the world, beheld suffering and misery. With pity He saw how men had become victims of satanic cruelty. He looked with compassion upon those who were being corrupted, murdered, and lost" (*The Desire of Ages*, p. 36).

Now I realized that the way I felt was undoubtedly a result of Christ's imparting His compassionate love to me by the Holy Spirit in answer to prayer. A sudden desire to stop and pray for them possessed me as I passed a supermarket. Turning into the parking area, I drove to the back, where I turned the motor off. As I did, I said to myself, "I only wish that our Lord had a special intensive care unit for those devastated by the ravages of sin and oppressed by Satan."

My wife, Hilda, a nurse, was at the time working in the intensive care unit of a large hospital. A couple days previously we had talked about her work, and I had been fascinated by the care and dedication the nurses exercised toward their patients. I longed for similar spiritual help for those facing crises.

Taking my Bible out of my briefcase, I opened it at the twenty-seventh chapter of Matthew and read some about the Crucifixion. Then I pleaded in prayer the merits of the blood that Christ had shed on Calvary as the reason that the man I had just talked to, and his wife, should receive divine help.

Suddenly I recalled a short article that I had read sometime back about divine power being available in times of need. It had been in one of the volumes of *Testimonies for the Church*. Again I reached into my briefcase and pulled out a volume. You see, I kept that briefcase with me day and night. It contained my Bible, the Conflict of the Ages Series, the *Testimonies for the Church* and *Christ's Object Lessons*, and other books. Since I never went to a restaurant but bought fruits and nuts to eat in my car, I always spent my lunch hour reading.

As it was a quarter till noon, I decided to take my lunch break. Looking for that article, I found it, beginning on page 19 of volume 8 of the *Testimonies*, under the title "The Power Promised": "God does not ask us to do in our own strength the work before us. He has provided divine assistance for all the emergencies to which our human resources are unequal. He gives the Holy Spirit to help in every strait, to strengthen our hope and assurance, to illuminate our minds and purify our hearts. . . . Christ has made provision that His church shall be a transformed body, illumined with the light of heaven, possessing the glory of Immanuel. It is His purpose that every Christian shall be surrounded with a spiritual atmosphere of light and peace."

Then I figured that a God-loving, dedicated Christian would not be satisfied with just basking in that spiritual atmosphere of light and peace, but would go out and bring in the poor in righteousness, the lame and the maimed that have had head-on collisions with sin, and those oppressed by Satan, and have them all surrounded with that same spiritual environment.

The first paragraph of the quotation made a special impact upon me as I read it over a number of times. As I meditated upon it I recalled a statement found on page 671 of *The Desire of Ages* that stated that God's Holy Spirit is the only means by which we can resist and overcome sin. Only the Holy Spirit can give us victory over self, over the world, and over evil angels.

"In describing to His disciples the office work of the Holy Spirit, Jesus sought to inspire them with the joy and hope that inspired His own heart. He rejoiced because of the abundant help He had provided for His church. The Holy Spirit was the highest of all gifts that He could solicit from His Father for the exaltation of His people. The Spirit was to be given as a regenerating agent, and without this the sacrifice of Christ would have been of no avail. The power of evil had been strengthening for centuries, and the submission of men to this satanic captivity was amazing. Sin could be resisted and overcome only through the mighty agency of the third person of the Godhead, who would come with no modified energy, but in the fullness of divine power. It is the Spirit that makes effectual what has been wrought out by the world's Redeemer. It is by the Spirit that the heart is made pure. . . . Christ has given His Spirit as a divine power to overcome all hereditary and cultivated tendencies to evil."

Now I became deeply convinced that my prayers for others were of little value if I did not fervently ask for the mighty power of the third person of the Godhead to work miracles of redemption in the lives of those I prayed for.

As Jesus rejoiced over the abundant help He had provided for His church, in like manner my heart thrilled as I saw and understood what the Holy Spirit could do to transform others. An additional bit of information found on page 20 of volume 8 of the *Testimonies* completed the picture in my mind of the provision Jesus had made for sin-sick individuals to receive God's intensive care of the Holy Spirit. And I discovered that the help is available right now.

"To us today, as verily as to the first disciples, the promise of the Spirit belongs. . . . At this very hour His Spirit and His grace
are for all who need them and will take Him at His word."

God was leading me into a prayer ministry that would bless the lives of a great many persons, bringing them the peace of His love in a cruel world.

The time I had taken to have the businessman tell me about his problems God helped me to make up that afternoon. On every call I found owners at their business, in a good mood, and interested in having a larger and better yellow pages program. At the end of the day I totaled my increase and found it to be the best day in net revenue I had ever had. It greatly pleased my supervisor, who asked me to pass on the secret of my success to the other advertising representatives. I did by saying that the great Monarch of the galaxies had crowned my efforts with His divine blessing.

To secure divine help for the body shop man and his wife, I lived the next two weeks a bit differently. Each night I set the alarm clock 15 minutes earlier than usual because I wanted to begin each new day with prayer for the couple. After reconsecrating and rededicating my life to God, I would intercede with Him in their behalf. With the Bible opened at the Crucifixion chapter, Matthew 27, I pleaded the merits of Christ's blood as the reason that they should receive special help in their daily lives.

My first intercession went something like this: "Precious heavenly Father, I wish to thank Thee first for having allowed Christ to come and live among us and then purchase our redemption at such a great cost. In addition, I desire to express my appreciation in that You have honored me so greatly before the inhabitants of the galaxies and the angels of heaven by having made me a member of Jesus' resistance forces in a sin-occupied world.

"I also rejoice over the fact that You have blessed Your commandment-keeping church with the gift of the Spirit of Prophecy, thereby revealing unto us the many functions the Holy Spirit can perform to work out human salvation, and close Thy mission on earth with power and great glory. Gracious Father, because the pen of inspiration has referred to Thee as 'the Father of infinite pity,' I do not hesitate to bring to Your attention the lives of Mr. and Mrs. A.

"I realize that they have been under the constant attack of Satan and have struggled with depressing thoughts and experiences. Yes, their lives are in a sad state of affairs, and I refuse to sit back and do nothing while God's enemies increase their efforts to defeat Christ's work in man's behalf, and to fasten souls in their snares.

"I plead, O Lord, the merits of the blood the Lord of glory shed on Calvary for the remission of sins, for the salvation of this couple. You know, Father, that I do not hesitate to ask for the divine power of the third person of the Godhead to rebuke Lucifer and his spirit associates from controlling human lives. When I was a spiritist, the persevering supplications of Cyril and Cynthia Grosse in my behalf opened the way for Thy Holy

Spirit to shelter me from demonic activities for a whole week, making it possible for me to receive Bible studies and accept Christ as my Lord and Saviour.

"So, Father, may Thy Holy Spirit overshadow Mr. and Mrs. A this day, surrounding them with a spiritual atmosphere of light and peace, allowing them to make intelligent decisions in this present life and for eternity. I know, Lord, that You will not force anyone into a particular course of action, but You are able to help people in making right decisions.

"Nor do I hesitate to ask for mighty miracles of divine grace to take place in their lives, since Christ has already paid the price for any and all blessings that heaven can bestow.

"As for myself, as an intercessor in opening the way for the third person of the Godhead to move in mighty ways for them, I would appreciate seeing my prayers answered before my eyes when I return to see the man in two weeks, and may an overflow of the Spirit's blessings shower upon me so that I will be able to say like Job of old: 'When the ear heard me, then it blessed me; and when the eye saw me, it gave witness to me: because I delivered the poor that cried, and the fatherless, and him that had none to help him. The blessing of him that was ready to perish came upon me' [Job 29:11-13].

"And Father, may this experience bring me closer to my Saviour, 'that I may know him [better], and the power of his resurrection' [Philippians 3:10]. Lord God, as this intercession comes to a close, let it not be the end, but the beginning, of a precious walk with Thee. Again, I thank Thee for Thy love and Thy grace so preciously dispensed in the lives of those I pray for.

"This petition I present in the name of our merciful and faithful High Priest, Christ Jesus, who has acquired the legal right, in the sight of the inhabitants of the galaxies and the angels of heaven, to appropriate to the fallen descendants of Adam His great righteousness and complete salvation."

Two weeks passed, and with mixed feelings I entered Mr. A's place of business. While I expected to hear of blessings received, it was also possible that the couple could have resisted the leading of the Spirit of God in exercising their God-given right of freedom of choice and have made wrong decisions. But it wasn't long before I realized that things were looking up in their lives.

Stepping into the doorway of the bookkeeper's office, I asked if Mr. A was going to be tied up very long with the man in his office. The bookkeeper stated that I would be able to see him in a few minutes, then invited me to sit down. He added that his boss had just finalized plans to have the shop enlarged. Furthermore, the businessman had been expecting me to stop by that morning. Instantly I lifted up my heart to God in a silent melody of praise as I began to see that the power of His love had been benefiting those I had prayed for.

Mr. A greeted me with a firm handshake and a peaceful expression reflecting God's love. "I have a lot of good news to tell you. Things that are almost unbelievable have taken place since you were here. My wife and I are on good terms again, and life has taken on a new meaning."

As he continued, I could tell that the Spirit of God had been working in their lives, as described on page 173 of The Desire of Ages: "When the Spirit of God takes possession of the heart, it transforms the life. . . . Love, humility, and peace take the place of anger, envy, and strife. Joy takes the place of sadness, and the countenance reflects the light of heaven."

He told me how for three days after I had stopped by his office his wife began acting differently. When he went home for lunch and the evening meal, he found to his surprise the TV turned off and their favorite classical music playing in the background. She was pleasant but seemed lost in her own thoughts. A couple days later she called him at the office and asked if he could work things out so that he wouldn't have to return to the shop after dinner. The man stated that he could, but would probably get home a bit later than usual.

At home she treated him to a candlelight dinner. Then she explained that she had been giving serious thought to the tensions that had threatened their marriage. She now believed herself capable of taking control of her life and stated that she had matured in a few short days from a confused mess to a calm, reasonable person. Furthermore she added that life was too short to waste feeling sorry for oneself when in reality she had so much to be thankful for.

As he described to me what he called his good fortune, my heart thrilled with a joy born of heaven, and silently I thanked and praised the Holy Trinity for making me a channel for "the outflowing of the highest influence in the universe" (*Testimonies*, vol. 8, p. 22).

He then stated how he himself had experienced a few days of self-examination. Both of them had decided to venture on what one could call a new beginning.

"This may be hard for you to believe, but I am telling you without exaggeration that the whole atmosphere of our home has changed," he concluded. "I don't know how to explain it. It's so peaceful, so enjoyable. Coming home is a pleasant experience again."

Now he was making new plans for the business. He figured that if he were to enlarge the building some and get two additional auto body repairmen, the added revenues would enable him to hire a qualified person to make repair estimates and manage the place. Then he would be able to take some time off every so often, and spend it with his wife.

"How do you explain something so fantastic taking place in so short a time?" he suddenly asked.

Silently, I prayed, "Heavenly Father, please bless my mind with the right thing to say."

Aloud I said, "Mr. A, if you recall, as I left here two weeks ago, I mentioned that I would remember you and your wife in my prayers. Well, what you have experienced is the result of answered prayers."

Shaking his head, he replied, "I believe you, and appreciate greatly your having prayed for us, but I have never seen prayers answered with such power. The Mrs. and I are church-going people, but I must admit that I have never seen prayers answered this way—prayers that actually change lives."

To my surprise, his expression and voice suddenly slipped into a note of desperation. "Please, please promise me that you will continue praying for us, please!"

Never in my life had I felt so needed by someone, and at the same time so glad that I was seeing my prayers answered.

"Mr. A, I promise to pray for you and your wife. In fact, I will place your names on my perpetual prayer list. I will see to it that daily intercessions will ascend to God in your behalf."

With the pressure of my schedule in mind, I quickly revised his ad, then left for my next call. I did not work that telephone directory the following year, as I had graduated to major markets, but I met at a regional meeting the fellow who had handled the account, and received some good news.

"Roger, Mr. A sends you his regards. He wanted me to tell you about the success of his business, and above all, that everything is well with the family. In fact, he said that things have never been better at home. He didn't tell me what you men talked about, but somehow you have made a profound impression upon the man."

It was indeed good news to hear that the Spirit of God was giving intensive care to the couple on a daily basis.

CHAPTER
5

Prayers With High Dividends

It wasn't long after the Hudson, Ohio, experience that a statement on page 495 of *The Desire of Ages* caught my attention in a special way. "The science of salvation cannot be explained; but it can be known by experience."

The passage stuck in my mind. As I meditated upon the matter, read the Bible, and prayed about it, asking that God's Holy Spirit would give me insights on the subject, God answered my prayers, and within a period of two years His Spirit led me into a number of experiences that brought me the insights I had prayed for. Then it became very clear that prayers sprinkled with the blood of Christ were an entering wedge that can force ajar, then throw wide open, the massive gates of Satan's citadel.

They bring in the mighty power of the Holy Spirit that alone can immobilize the forces of darkness, unshackle spiritual captives, and lead them to freedom in Christ. Permit me to explain.

For many years I had meditated upon the experience of the apostle Paul. It amazed me that Jesus had appeared to the man on his way to Damascus to point out that his religious zeal was misguided.

Think of it—the Lord of glory talking to a man who hurled believers into prison, was instrumental in having many put to death, and even found pleasure in trying to force some of them to blaspheme (Acts 26:10, 11).

Questions kept running through my mind. Why would God follow such a course with Saul of Tarsus? Was He showing favoritism toward Saul by working for his salvation in a manner different from what He was willing to do to save other men into His eternal kingdom?

Then one day as I was sitting in my car waiting in a long line in front of a car wash, an answer came loud and clear. I had my Bible open, reading 1 Timothy 2: "I exhort therefore, that, first of all, supplications, prayers, intercessions, and giving of thanks, be made for all men; for kings, and for all that are in authority. . . . For this is good and acceptable in the sight of God our Saviour; who will have all men to be saved, and to come unto the knowledge of the truth." Instantly a paragraph found in volume 7 of the *Testimonies* that I had memorized long ago came to mind with a whole new understanding.

"We do not understand as we should the great conflict going on between invisible agencies, the controversy between loyal and disloyal angels. Over every man, good and evil angels strive. This is no make-believe conflict. It is not mimic battles in which we are engaged. We have to meet most powerful adversaries, and it rests with us to determine which shall win. We are to find our strength where the early disciples found theirs. . . . 'These all continued with one accord in prayer and supplication' " (p. 213).

Up to that time I had understood the words "and it rests with us to determine which shall win" as strictly relating to one's own personal experience. But now I saw those words to mean the experiences of others as well.

I began to see the great importance Paul attached to the power of intercessory prayer in the salvation of the ungodly. A couple days earlier I had read for my morning devotions the nineteenth chapter of Acts and Ellen White's commentary on it entitled "Ephesus" in *The Acts of the Apostles*. I saw how Paul found himself with a dozen young believers in the city of Ephesus, the capital of a major province of the Roman Empire.

"Ephesus was not only the most magnificent, but the most corrupt, of the cities of Asia" (*The Acts of the Apostles*, p. 286). Secular history establishes Ephesus as one of the great occult centers of the ancient Roman Empire.

Paul must have done some serious praying, and the power of the Spirit of God "wrought special miracles by the hands of Paul" (Acts 19:11). "And the name of the Lord Jesus was magnified" (verse 17). The power of Satan over the people shattered, then psychics, astrologers, fortunetellers, and spirit worshipers converted to Christ Jesus. They brought their books on the occult and "burned them before all men; and they counted the price of them, and found it fifty thousand pieces of silver" (verse 19).

A definite picture began to form in my mind about Paul's exhortations to Timothy, who at the time was pastor of the church at Ephesus, laboring to convert the Ephesians solidly established in a pagan culture. I concluded that conversions to Christianity were to be made through prayer and supplication to God.

Then I saw and understood clearly why Jesus had worked in the way He did to call Saul of Tarsus to Christianity. Someone had been praying for Saul's conversion. Not one day had passed without that person pleading to God.

I can imagine that whoever it was remembered the words of Jesus, "I say unto you, Love your enemies, bless them that curse you, do good to them that hate you, and pray for them which despitefully use you, and persecute you" (Matthew 5:44).

The person was undoubtedly obsessed with a deep conviction that prayers sprinkled with the precious blood of Christ would permit the arm of the Almighty to move in special ways for Saul's conversion to Christianity. While I am sure that most believers mentioned Saul in their prayers, it was that in some way, somehow, God would stop him from persecuting them.

On the other hand, this special person was praying with one objective in mind: Saul's conversion. And one day a neighbor knocked at his or her door and said, "Let me in; I have some great news to tell you. It's almost unbelievable, but Saul of Tarsus has become a Christian." And after the details were told, that person probably did not seem surprised, and may have said, "I knew all the time that sooner or later the Lord of glory was going to save Saul from himself. I have been praying quite a while for his conversion."

What an answer to prayer that was. God after having listened to such prayers for some time saw that He could answer them in only one way. He would have to talk to Saul personally, flashing forth His divine majesty.

Miracles Are Coming

It is my belief that mighty miracles of redemption will soon take place through the power of intercessory prayer as the Holy Spirit leads vast numbers of God's people into such a prayer ministry for the unsaved.

Ellen White declared a hundred years ago that "before the final visitation of God's judgments upon the earth there will be among the people of the Lord such a revival of primitive godliness as has not been witnessed since apostolic times" (The Great Controversy, p. 464).

I understand her statement to mean that God's people will return to basics. They will take Paul's advice to Timothy seriously, and put it into daily practice. "I exhort therefore, that, first of all, supplications, prayers, intercessions, and giving of thanks, be made for all men."

In other words, persevering supplications to God in faith for the unsaved, the ungodly, will ascend to the mercy seat daily. People will cry to the "Father of infinite pity" for Him to appropriate the merits of the blood of Christ shed on Calvary for sinners to the individuals they pray for. We will then see miracles of redemption as the Spirit of God transforms people.

I have seen the blood of Christ work wonders in people's lives. In fact, I have felt that power working in my own. "The science of salvation cannot be explained; but it can be known by experience." We don't understand how redemption works through the shed blood of Christ, but we can witness it in operation. Permit me to illustrate by glancing back for a few moments on my conversion from spiritism.

It almost causes me to tremble when I think how close I came to missing out on eternal life. Had it not been for Cyril and Cynthia Grosse interceding in my behalf, pleading the merits of the blood of Christ to atone for my sins, believing that the Holy Spirit could overrule the forces of evil and bring deliverance, I would not be rejoicing today in the hope of eternal life.

There I was, a man that conversed with demonic spirits. Thoughts of God were the farthest things from my mind. But I had promised my Jewish boss that I would find out for him why Cyril Grosse, being a Christian, observed the seventh-day Sabbath. What I did not realize at the time was that the Grosses were people of prayer who prayed for an ungodly individual with a firm belief that the Holy Spirit could work out my salvation.

From the beginning I told them that I had no interest in religion, being a confirmed atheist. All I wanted was for them to show me from the Bible what they based their Christian observance of the seventh-day Sabbath on. "And by the way," I said, "does the Bible have much to say about the supernatural world of spirits?"

From that moment on the Spirit of God moved upon my mind with power. After five days of studying the Bible four hours per evening, I made a decision for Christ, observed the biblical Sabbath the following day, then told the couple about my affiliation with spirit worship. They stated that something about me had disturbed them.

A few days later the spirits tried to destroy them with a flash fire that instantly turned their living room into an inferno. Trapped behind a wall of flame, Cynthia's only escape was a window that overlooked a drop of three stories.

Cyril ran for a blanket to throw to her, while her brother phoned the fire department. When her husband returned seconds later, Cynthia stood in the doorway. A powerful voice had told her to jump through the fire. The ends of the hair on her head were singed, her eyelashes were burned, and yet the flames had not touched any part of her body or clothing.

After the firemen had put out the fire, they found that the spot where Cynthia had been standing had exploded with such force that it blew a hole through the ceiling. Everything in the room had burned. And in the closet a strange phenomenon had taken place. A suitcase with clothing in it had escaped the flames, yet some of the clothing inside were ashes while the rest remained intact. The firemen had never seen anything like it before.

That experience served, at the very beginning of my Christian walk, to create in me an awareness of the power of intercessory prayer. I had been praying fervently for them after the demons had declared that I, along with the young couple who had given me Bible studies, would go to an early grave. Daily my prayers now ascended to God for His loving care over them.

Cyril and Cynthia Grosse presently reside in California, where for many years they have been educators with the Los Angeles school system.

Now let me return to my experience in front of the car wash. I became deeply impressed with the thought that God was calling me to do a work that not even the angels of heaven could do. He wanted me to be an intercessor for the unsaved and the ungodly that I met in my work. And I knew exactly where to find the power to help such people—in prayer and supplication to God, who waits for our requests for help so that He will then have the legal right in the sight of the inhabitants of the universe to move with power into Satan's domain and rescue his captives.

I need to clarify the expression "the unsaved and the ungodly." Often they are highly intelligent, refined, and cultured individuals who are successful in the business world. They are law-abiding citizens looked upon with great admiration and respect. But when it comes to their spiritual well-being, they lack everything.

In addition, you will find many prosperous people who by their gutter language reveal that they are truly ungodly, and have a way of life that they do not care to change. In both groups, many, though well off financially, are carrying heavy burdens. Some even sow distress and misery in the lives of others because the perplexities of their own lives pressure them into being mean and cruel.

In the fall of 1968 my company assigned me to work the Buffalo, New York, telephone directory, and I did so for several years. That vast market area brought me in contact with great and influential people, including presidents of large corporations. I became well acquainted with them because of the many times I met with them every year to restructure their large telephone directory advertising programs.

Here is where I saw God's Holy Spirit work in wonderful ways. But before recounting some of my prayer experiences, I feel it's important to consider the frame of mind that motivated Jesus as He prayed for human beings.

Ellen White has revealed the all-powerful element that compelled Christ to go to Calvary: "Love for God, zeal for His glory, and love for fallen humanity, brought Jesus to earth to suffer and to die. This was the controlling power in His life. This principle He bids us adopt" (*The Desire of Ages*, p. 330).

As I have read the Bible and the writings of Ellen White over the years, I have observed that our Lord tried constantly to impress the minds of His disciples with His divine compassionate love for fallen mortals. He spent much time in prayer, giving them an example to follow so that they also could become mighty intercessors for others.

When He ascended to heaven He had no fear that His disciples would fail Him as they worked for the salvation of others. He would send them the One who would teach them how to live in such a way as not to fail their Redeemer.

I have found nine essential factors behind successful, victorious, Christian living. When through the Holy Spirit we possess them, we can then ask God that the same blessings may crown the lives of those we pray for. Let's consider those factors closely.

Factor 1

Ellen White reveals that this factor constitutes the very foundation of God's government (*The Great Controversy*, p. 493). In fact, *divine compassionate love* flows directly from the heart of God. It is a love for others that knows no bounds.

While human love is wrapped up in selfishness and produces results that are at best shaky and short-lived, divine compassionate love is a force that never fails. I find great comfort in the fact that the "Father of infinite pity" so loved humanity that "he gave his only begotten Son, that whosoever believeth in him should not perish, but have everlasting life."

We need to hunger and thirst for God to impart that divine force to us. In talking about the love of Christ and our great need of it, Ellen White observed that "the completeness of Christian character is attained when the impulse to help and bless others springs constantly from within" (*Christ's Object Lessons*, p. 384).

It is my firm conviction that the reason that Christian homes are breaking up as they are today, devastating the lives of men, women, and children, is that our Christian hearts lack that divine compassionate love. We may not admit it, but the results are speaking louder than words.

Factor 2

The next factor is often greatly misunderstood because of a powerful counterfeit. That valuable element is *heavenly joy*.

Through the ages Satan has mislead humans by causing them to believe that they will find joy in self-pleasing and self-serving. And that they can obtain it without consideration for others. But such a lifestyle leads only to disappointment and often great unhappiness.

On the other hand, we will find a joy that never fails in Christ. "Those who abide in Jesus will be happy, cheerful, and joyful in God" (*Testimonies*, vol. 4, p. 626).

Romans 15:3 says that "Christ pleased not himself." He found great joy in blessing the lives of others. "Not for Himself, but for others, He lived and thought and prayed" (*Christ's Object Lessons*, p. 139).

About the early disciples the Bible declares, "And the disciples were filled with joy, and with the Holy Ghost" (Acts 13:52).

I believe that today we need to pray for heavenly joy with great intensity and desire. Only then can we work to pass the same blessing to others.

Factor 3

Both the rich and the poor and the strong and the weak seek peace. Because there are various degrees of peace, I like to reach out for the very best—that is, *heavenly peace*. That kind of peace brings pleasant relaxation by imparting a mental or spiritual state of mind that frees us from disquieting and perturbing fears.

We think of Jesus, who slept in a boat during a storm (Mark 4:38-40), or of Peter, who slept soundly during the night before his scheduled execution (Acts 12:6; *Acts of the Apostles*, p. 146).

We today need that same freedom from fear. How can a person acquire such a state of mind? When the Comforter, the Holy Spirit, the representative of Christ on earth, imparts heavenly peace to someone, He completely delivers that person's mind from any fears that would make him or her anxious or restless.

Factor 4

To appreciate this factor, one has to remember the cruel world that we live in. Distresses and perplexities come in many forms, but the most difficult ones are the injustices and unkindness inflicted upon us by others. Sometimes it amounts to harsh and even cruel treatment by individuals who have no control of their tongues.

The apostle James in chapter 3 of his Epistle compares the human tongue to a little fire that turns into an inferno doing vast damage. To survive such experiences one has to receive special help in the form of *longsuffering*, another divine attribute of our Redeemer. When God met with Moses on Mount Sinai, He declared Himself to be "the Lord God, merciful and gracious, longsuffering, and abundant in goodness and truth" (Exodus 34:6).

If we seek a fresh baptism of this heavenly grace on a daily basis, we will be able to put up with the shortcomings of others, and sincerely pray for a divine blessing on their lives also. Then like the apostle Paul we will be able to say, "I can do all things through Christ which strengtheneth me" (Philippians 4:13).

Factor 5

Here we have an element of great value to those engaged

in the field of communication. Be it in the business world or in working directly with people who need help, a most valuable asset is *gentleness.*

Ellen White reminds us that even God is impressed by it, and looks upon it with admiration. "True gentleness is a gem of great value in the sight of God" (*Testimonies,* vol. 3, p. 536). Jesus beautifully illustrated it during His ministry on earth, and He always accompanied it with the element of tact.

Webster's Dictionary defines tact as "that delicate perception of the right thing to say or do without offending." Ellen White spoke of divine tact and gentleness (*Testimonies,* vol. 6, p. 400).

I was working on the Buffalo, New York, telephone directory for the third year, and the canvass had begun but a few days before. One morning my sales manager told me to come into his office before going out on my calls. Naturally I wondered what was so important that he wouldn't talk about it at my desk.

As I entered his office he asked me to close the door, then phoned the receptionist to say that he would not take any calls until he told her. My heart sank into my chest, since I knew whenever he did that, it spelled trouble. But I regained my composure when he said that he would like me to do him a favor. The conversation went something like this.

"Roger, I have here the files of a large account that needs very special care, and that should be handled by someone who is tactful and at the same time has the patience of an angel, or close to it. This ticket adds up to several hundreds of dollars in monthly billing. As we managers were setting up the assignments for the 43 of you, this account received a lot of discussion as to who was best suited to handle it. We need someone with the finesse, the tact, the expertise to make a favorable impression on the client. Roger, I believe that you are the right man for the job."

"What about the person who had it last year?"

"We cannot let him handle it again, seeing that he had a very difficult time with it. The account was closed 10 days before the book was shipped to the printers, with a loss of almost $200 per month in billing. Our man says that the president of the corporation is most difficult to talk to. He just will not set up an appointment to go over his yellow pages advertising program. Instead he told the rep to drop in two or three times a week until he finds him with some time to spare. The fellow claims that he went there more than 50 times over a period of six months."

As I sized up the situation, I felt extremely reluctant to accept the challenge, then silently prayed, "Jesus, what should I do?" Instantly a quotation came to mind: "When in faith we take hold of His strength, He will change, wonderfully change, the most hopeless, discouraging outlook. He will do this for the glory of His name" (*Testimonies*, vol. 8, p. 12). Then I knew that the Lord would be with me. I felt that it could turn out to be an occasion for all the managers, and the whole sales force, to see that the Lord God who said "Remember the sabbath day, to keep it holy" does take care of His people.

My boss reminded me of some difficult business calls he had made with me as an observer in the past, and how impressed he had been of the way I had handled them.

"Roger, I am aware that a great power accompanies you, and I would like the folks here to be made aware of it also. Will you take the challenge, and make me proud of you?"

"I can see that it will take a miracle from God to make a success of this undertaking, but trusting in His power, I believe all will turn out well. I will accept the assignment."

Within 10 days I had closed the account and increased the billing substantially. After praying that the Lord would give me divine tact and gentleness, I phoned for a five-minute appointment with the man, just to introduce myself, and got it on the spot. The positive first contact led to another interview a few days later, where I showed him some ads I had prepared. On that call he was pleased with the work I had done, and to my great surprise asked if I would be willing to see him at his office at 7:00 a.m. so that we could talk about some of his other businesses and additional advertising. The place would be quiet for him till about 9:00 a.m. I agreed to that.

During that interview, while I prepared the ads, he told me of the terrible problem he and his wife were having with their only son. The young man had been the joy of their lives until he became hooked on drugs and got into trouble with the law. They could hardly stand being disgraced that way. He added that the experience had somehow caused him to become unkind to others, something he found himself unable to change. As we conversed I promised to keep them in my daily prayers, which he thanked me for.

About a month later he called me to have a new product line included in his ads. During the conversation he stated that things were getting better at home, and to keep praying for them. I explained that he would have to sign new copy sheets to authorize the changes in his ads, so we set up an appointment for two days later.

As I was rearranging his ads, he told me of some interesting changes that had taken place involving his son. The boy had decided to change his lifestyle, and had sought his parents' help in the matter. The man's wife no longer needed powerful medications to help her nerves. He could sleep entire nights now, and the feeling of carrying the world on his shoulders had left him.

Then he said something that thrilled me. "My wife and I believe that your praying for us has brought great blessings into our lives. I told her that when you left my office a powerful presence of peace and joy remained with me that whole day."

Factor 6

Again we find an attribute of God, one that might frustrate us at first since the Bible clearly says that we do not have it. It is the element of *goodness*.

The prophet Jeremiah wrote that the human heart is "deceitful above all things, and desperately wicked" (Jeremiah 17:9). The ancient Hebrews failed God miserably because of their lack of goodness. Their unconsecrated lives led to their ruin. The prophet Ezekiel described the situation this way.

"Son of man, when the house of Israel dwelt in their own land, they defiled it by their own way and by their doings. . . . And I scattered them among the heathen, and they were dispersed through the countries. . . . And when they entered unto the heathen, thither they went, they profaned my holy name, when they said to them, These are the people of the Lord. . . . But I had pity for mine holy name. . . . Therefore say unto the house of Israel, Thus saith the Lord God; I do not this for your sakes, O house of Israel, but for mine holy name's sake. . . . I will sanctify my great name. . . . and the heathen shall know that I am the Lord, saith the Lord God, when I shall be sanctified *in you* before their eyes. . . . A new heart also will I give you, and a new spirit will I put within you. . . . I will put my spirit within you, and cause you to walk in my statutes, and ye shall keep my judgments, and do them" (Ezekiel 36:17-27).

It is a terrific encouragement to know that the Lord is more than eager to provide us with His goodness, and to enable us to experience successful, victorious, Christian living through the indwelling of His Holy Spirit if only we take the time to daily ask for it.

Factor 7

This factor is so vital to one's Christian experience that in its absence spiritual growth will not take place. In fact, the Bible tells us that without it, one cannot please God. That most important factor is a *living faith*.

"Without faith it is impossible to please him: for he that cometh to God must believe that he is, and that he is a rewarder of them that diligently seek him" (Hebrews 11:6).

A living faith is one that increases our spiritual strength, enabling us to develop an unfaltering trust in our heavenly Father, and in the power of His Holy Spirit. Mrs. White has opened before God's people the means by which we can obtain it. "Faith is inspired by the Holy Spirit, and will flourish only as it is cherished" (*The Great Controversy*, p. 527).

When a person prays for it, he or she might as well seek the highest degree of faith available. That is genuine biblical faith. It will impart great belief in God, great trust in Him, and above all, a loyalty to Him that will be *immovable*. The kind that we read about in the eleventh chapter of Hebrews.

Factor 8

In a world that promotes self-esteem and self-exaltation on

every side, God's people need as never before a precious heavenly trait that adorns the character of Christ. That valuable factor is the *meekness* of Christ.

To be unpretentious, humble, and submissive to God's will is of great value in God's sight. "Thus saith the high and lofty One that inhabiteth eternity, whose name is Holy; I dwell in the high and holy place, with him also that is of a contrite and humble spirit, to revive the spirit of the humble, and to revive the heart of the contrite ones" (Isaiah 57:15).

Factor 9

About a hundred years ago, Mrs. White, through divine inspiration, was told that at the very close of earth's history, immorality would abound everywhere, and licentiousness would be the special sin of the age. Jesus declared that "as the days of [Noah] were, so shall also the coming of the Son of man be." We read in Genesis 6:5 that "God saw that the wickedness of man was great in the earth, and that every imagination of the thoughts of his heart was only evil continually."

How can we expect to live a successful, victorious Christian life when we find ourselves surrounded with evil? Only by following Jesus' way. "Christ came to this world to show that by receiving power from on high, man can live an unsullied life" (*The Ministry of Healing*, p. 25). In other words, an unsoiled or undefiled life.

"Not even by a thought did he yield to temptation" (*The Desire of Ages*, p. 123). What is that special power that we need so greatly? It is *self-control* imparted by the Spirit of God.

An old turn-of-the-century dictionary of mine defines self-control as "the ability to check or regulate, to restrain, and to govern self in all aspects of life." We can possess purity of thought, purity of heart, and purity of life even in this day and age by controlling our thoughts with the power of the Spirit of God blessing our minds. Romans 12:21 tells us to "overcome evil with good." Keeping the mind busy with thoughts that will elevate and ennoble one's character is the formula to success here.

I have found by experience that an excellent way to do that

is to work at memorizing God's Holy Word. However, I am not the first person to have discovered that. "Thy word have I hid in mine heart, that I might not sin against thee," the psalmist said.

Failure to control one's thoughts can be disastrous. Writing about Samson, Ellen White said, "Physically, Samson was the strongest man upon the earth; but in self-control, integrity, and firmness, he was one of the weakest of men" (*Patriarchs and Prophets*, p. 567). And on the following page she tells us that the real greatness of a man is "measured by the power of the feelings that he controls."

The Word of God says of man, "As he thinketh in his heart, so is he" (Proverbs 23:7). "Who shall ascend into the hill of the Lord? or who shall stand in his holy place? He that hath clean hands, and a pure heart" (Psalm 24:3, 4).

I find great encouragement in these words: "Christ has given His Spirit as a divine power to overcome all hereditary and cultivated tendencies to evil, and to impress His own character upon His church" (*The Desire of Ages*, p. 671).

Victory through Christ—what a majestic experience!

Prayers that will produce high dividends for the kingdom of God are ours to experience and enjoy now.

C H A P T E R
6

A Perpetual
Prayer List

It was hay fever time, and having awakened at 4:00 a.m. with a fit of sneezing, I took some medication to alleviate the distress. As I realized that sleep had now escaped me, I asked the Lord to lead my mind into meditation and prayer. Immediately I began thinking about the fierce battle the children of Israel found themselves in when the Amalekites attacked them at Rephidim.

Moses, Aaron, and Hur observed the conflict from the top of a hill. Moses, the praying man that he was, stretched out his arms toward heaven, interceding for his people. The battle went in the Israelites' favor until Moses' hands became heavy and he had to put them down. Then the enemy began to prevail.

As the pattern repeated itself a couple more times, Aaron and Hur realized that they had to hold Moses' hands up toward heaven in order for Israel to be victorious. Taking a large stone, they sat their leader on it, then both of them held up his hands all day long till the sun went down and Israel had won the skirmish.

Thoughts of the incident led me to understand that in interceding for those in need, consistency in prayer is of greater importance than I had previously assumed. I recalled how my prayers for others over the years produced little results until I made myself a prayer list, and brought every person before the Lord daily. It was then that I began to see

67

many of my prayers answered before my eyes.

At that point numerous individuals gained victory over the power of sin as in answer to prayer God pushed back the forces of darkness so that they had a chance to think for themselves.

For example, Robert overcame drugs and is again rejoicing with God's people (see chapter 7). Daily without fail for almost three years I had brought the young man's case before the throne of grace, praying that the Holy Spirit would lead him to repentance and help him to make intelligent decisions for his present life and for eternity.

You see, I believe firmly that "we can no more repent without the Spirit of Christ to awaken the conscience than we can be pardoned without Christ" (Steps to Christ, p. 26). God does not violate anyone's freedom of choice, however. The Spirit of God does not force people into anything that they do not desire. He only shows them a better way of life, and invites them to experience real joy and peace. The choice is theirs to make under these most favorable conditions.

As I reflected that early morning upon the battle between Israel and the Amalekites, a quotation came to mind that had given me great encouragement at the beginning of my Christian walk. "Hearts that have been the battleground of the conflict with Satan, and that have been rescued by the power of love, are more precious to the Redeemer than are those who have never fallen" (Christ's Object Lessons, p. 118).

The thought that the Creator treasures human beings, who are struggling with the power of sin and are rescued by the power of love, more dearly than the unfallen inhabitants of the galaxies filled my heart with surging concern for others. Feeling a sense of responsibility similar to what a father feels about the well-being of his children, I asked myself, "If I were to die, who would plead for the merits of Christ to be appropriated to those on my prayer list?"

Another question popped into my mind: How could I assure that daily intercessions would be made for those who are now receiving help from the Holy Spirit, lest they once more become perplexed, distressed, and oppressed?

With a sense of helplessness, I told myself, "What I need is some kind of perpetual prayer list." I don't know why I said that, but I did, and the thought stuck in my mind.

As a result, I began telling the Lord about my worry that my intercessions could cease suddenly, leaving others deprived of much-needed help.

For the previous couple days I had been memorizing passages from the seventeenth chapter of the Gospel of John about Jesus' great concern for His disciples. From them I knew that He understood the full extent of my concern for my people's needs.

"And now I am no more in the world, but these are in the world, and I come to thee. Holy Father, keep through thine own name those whom thou hast given me. . . . I pray not that thou shouldest take them out of the world, but that thou shouldest keep them from the evil. . . . Neither pray I for these alone, but for them also which shall believe on me through their word" (John 17:11-20).

Christ's words of intercession, encompassing all Christians to the end of time, led me to respond, "Dear Saviour, please make me a wise intercessor for my fellow humans so that the very best of our Father's blessings may crown their lives, leading them to the City of God."

Having spoken that short request, I waited for an answer. And to my great surprise, one came in the form of a quotation that I had memorized in 1947. (I recall the year because of an important event that had prompted me to memorize the short passage.) "Those who beg at midnight for loaves to feed the hungry souls will be successful."

Joy welled up in my heart. "Thank You, Lord, for the inspiration." Then I recalled that the quotation appeared on the same page of *Christ's Object Lessons* as the one on which Mrs. White speaks of a rainbow of promise encircling the throne of God.

Turning the light on, I pulled the book out of my night table drawer to read it again. I did not realize just then that the Lord was leading me there to find the answer to my perpetual prayer list. Just above the passage I had remembered, I read these words: "Like Aaron, who symbolized Christ, our Saviour bears the names of all His people on His heart in the holy place" (p. 148). Exodus 28:29 declares, "Aaron shall bear the names of the children of Israel in the breastplate of judgment upon his heart, when he goeth in unto the holy place, for a memorial before the Lord continually."

Here was the answer to my human limitations. I would have the Lord engrave the names of the many persons on my prayer list upon the breastplate of His righteousness. Were I to die that day, Jesus, the divine Intercessor, would continue to intercede by the mercy seat for them.

Yes, I indeed have a perpetual prayer list. And although over the decades it has grown to hundreds of individuals, the vastness of their needs has not burdened the Great Intercessor. The apostle Paul confidently wrote, "We have not an high priest which cannot be touched with the feeling of our infirmities; but was in all points tempted like as we are, yet without sin. Let us therefore come boldly unto the throne of grace, that we may obtain mercy, and find grace to help in time of need" (Hebrews 4:15, 16).

During the early seventies, while I was working on the Buffalo, New York, telephone directory, my superiors asked me if I was willing to help out in an emergency. The Plattsburgh, New York, telephone canvass was in progress, and a need had arisen for someone that could handle large business accounts, many of them located in Montreal, Canada. It would involve about a month.

I obliged, and tackled the project with vigor. With the divine power of the Holy Spirit opening the way before me, the undertaking turned out to be a great success. In fact, that year I was one of two men given special recognition in New York State, and honored by being made a member of the Sales Achievement Club for outstanding sales performances in yellow pages advertising.

After having called on business accounts in Montreal all day and driven the 60 miles back to Plattsburgh, I arrived at the office about 7:00 in the evening. I quickly posted on the canvass status board the amount of revenue handled that day, and the net gain in advertising dollars. Just then a fellow by the name of Anthony came in to post his report also. He had had an early evening appointment with a building contractor that had prevented him from eating at his regular time, so we decided to have our evening meal together.

As we were eating, Tony asked a couple questions about my wife and children. A few minutes later he told about his family life.

Again in this case, I saw the Holy Spirit inviting me to include the man in my prayer ministry. Tony was filled with remorse over an incident that had brought tragedy into the lives of several people. It had resulted in the loss of a successful business built up over many years of hard work, and had caused estrangement from his teenage children, whom he loved very much.

It began at a banking firm's Christmas party. He was conversing with the president of the bank and his secretary when the girl who had brought the latter said that because of a call from home she had to leave earlier than intended. Could the secretary get a ride back with someone else? At that moment Tony offered to help.

During the long drive to her place the secretary did most of the talking, and as he listened, the thought entered his mind that he should try to get a kiss for his trouble. He politely asked if she would object to a friendly Christmas kiss. To his great surprise she stated that it was an excellent idea, adding that she had been hoping for a little romance.

That supposedly innocent Christmas kiss turned out to be his undoing. The woman was also married, but had occasionally flirted with Tony when he visited the bank. The Christmas kiss was followed by a New Year's kiss, and developed into an affair.

After a few months of meeting at various motels, the woman's husband had her followed by a private investigator. Furious, the husband phoned Tony's wife to inform her of what had been going on. She in turn went into a rage that led her to demand a divorce settlement that wiped Tony out financially.

He had to sell his business to meet the legal fees and to satisfy the decision of the courts. He and his girlfriend decided to leave town and go to a big city. After working hard for three years at establishing themselves in what they called "their new lives," an unexpected event shattered all their dreams for the future.

The woman's husband contacted her and pleaded for her to return home for the sake of the children. She jumped at the offer, and left Tony so quickly that it stunned him senseless for days.

He tried to escape from his problems through drink. Now he spent his weekends in an alcoholic haze to escape his guilt.

I asked him if he had ever thought of seeking divine help.

"To be honest with you, Roger, I must say that I have no use for spiritual things. In fact, I have not been in a church since I was married, which was years ago."

A couple more questions revealed his almost total lack of knowledge about God and the Bible and his apparent satisfaction with his ignorance. He believed in God as a creative moving force that animates all forms of life, but refused to accept anything that had to do with a personal God.

Then I did something that shocked him. "Tony, seeing that you initiated this conversation and willingly told me about your problems, I want you to know that from this day on, I will be interceding in prayer for you. In fact, I will place your name on my prayer list, never to be removed. And I believe that the Holy Spirit will lead your feet to the City of God."

For a few seconds he was speechless. "I—I—I have never heard anything like that. I don't know just how to express myself here, but I want you to know that—that I am surprised and moved by your interest. The sincerity and power of your convictions, I must admit, have touched me, giving me a strange new feeling. I thank you for what you said." Then he changed the subject.

Because of our busy schedules, we did not have occasion to talk again except for a few words at the office. At the end of my assignment as I was leaving the office on Friday, he accompanied me to the car.

It was then that he made a statement that helped me

understand why my commitment to pray for him had so startled him.

"The reason that I was moved so deep'y. and almost lost control of my emotions in the presence of everybody in the restaurant, was because I had heard my grandmother say similar things. When I said that I had never heard words like those, what I meant to say was that I had never heard anything like that since my grandmother died. Before she passed away she said to me, 'Anthony, I believe that my prayers for you will be answered, and that the Spirit of God will lead your feet to the City of God.' "

As we parted, he said, "Roger, if ever my life gets straightened out and I become interested in spiritual things, I want you to know that I will be a Seventh-day Adventist. I have heard a lot of good things about Adventists."

Nine years passed before I met him again. By that time I had been promoted to division sales manager and was visiting a telephone directory canvass in Pennsylvania. One day at noon a couple of my men and I were looking the menu over in a restaurant when someone to my left said, "Roger Morneau, what brings you to this part of the world?"

When I looked up, there stood Tony with his hand extended in greeting. Now the area manager for a large marketing firm, he was with some of his men also, and they were just leaving. He stated that he would like to talk to me and would return in a few minutes and wait in his car until I finished my meal.

As we sat in the car, the very first thing that he did was remind me of our conversation nine years before in a Plattsburgh, New York, restaurant, and how it had been instrumental in getting him to think about those things that have real value in life. Thanking me several times for praying for him, he explained that he no longer used alcohol, had quit smoking, and above all, had become interested in spiritual matters because of some unusual outworkings of divine providence. Presently he was studying SDA beliefs with an Adventist couple on weekends.

After we parted, all day long I kept thanking and praising

Jesus for having led me to understand more fully the power of His ministration in the Holy of Holies of the heavenly sanctuary. Otherwise I would never have experienced the blessing that was mine to know that I have a perpetual prayer list in His carrying the names of all my people upon His heart.

C H A P T E R

7

Interceding for Young People

In the previous chapter I stated that a young man by the name of Robert obtained victory over drugs and returned to God's commandment-honoring people as the result of intercessory prayer in his behalf. I would like to tell you a bit more about his experience, and how the Spirit of God cared for and blessed his life during the time he had drifted away from God.

It was a sad surprise to learn from one of Robert's former college buddies the almost unbelievable changes that had taken place in the young man's life. In a few short years he had gone from being a God-loving young person to one dedicated to total self-centeredness.

"Robert," his college friend said, "is no longer the sharp young Christian you knew him to be. After college he found employment that brought him material prosperity, and in addition his wife's income placed them on easy street.

"They made friends with some of the people they were working with, which gradually led them into places of entertainment that they had not known before. The wife became fascinated by the music, and before long they were both hooked on rock. They occupied their leisure time with activities that not only separated them from God, but eventually from one another. Whether he left her or she left him, I don't exactly know."

The college friend added, "His brother told me that Robert

has a thousand dollars' worth of grass and other powerful stuff in his place. He spends hours smoking grass, and he loves heavy rock. In fact, he has sunk thousands of dollars into a top-notch stereo set to create the impression of being near the stage of a rock concert."

When I expressed my disappointment, the young man replied, "Don't feel bad about him. He knew better than to get himself involved in that type of situation. It's obviously what he wanted, or he would have stayed away from it from the beginning."

Naturally I immediately determined to take Robert's case before our heavenly Father on a daily basis. Knowing that sin can be "resisted and overcome only through the mighty agency of the third person of the Godhead" (*The Desire of Ages*, p. 671), I prayed that the Holy Spirit would bring Robert victory over rock music, liquor, and drugs. Naturally I realized that it could possibly take years before the man could reach a position where he could make decisions that would lead back to God, but I was prepared to pray for him the rest of my life.

Three years went by; then one day I had a lovely surprise. I met Robert on the grounds of Union Springs Academy as we were attending the annual New York Conference camp meeting. The next day I had the joy of hearing from him how the Spirit of God had worked in his behalf.

"It was about a year ago," he told me, "when I began to experience a change in the way I reasoned regarding my friends, my leisure time, my musical preferences, and other aspects of my daily life. Up to that time I had spurned spiritual things, and for a period of five years had given myself up to enjoying what the world calls the good life.

"From the time that I got up each morning to when I retired at night I was either involved in some form of self-gratification or living in anticipation of it. For instance, the very first thing I did each morning was to play some of my favorite rock music as I got ready for work. There was something about it that satisfied an inner craving.

"Every weekend was taken up with a wild party roaring with women, liquor, grass, and whatever else could liven it up. By then my wife and I had parted ways, and I was completely free to do whatever I wanted. And I loved it that way. But suddenly I came face to face with reality."

"Would you mind telling me about it?" I asked.

"About a year ago things began to change. First, my rock music and my beer went flat on me. One evening when I arrived home from work, I turned on the stereo set, placed a stack of favorite records on the turntable, then sat comfortably with a glass of my favorite beer in one hand and a newspaper in the other. I took a couple sips from the glass and read a few minutes, but when I had a third sip, I sensed that something had gone wrong. That mouthful of beer tasted bad. In fact, it was awful.

"I went to the refrigerator for another can, and after opening it, I found that it tasted worse than the first one. And the music was not the same—something was missing. It wasn't enjoyable as it had been, so I checked the controls on the amplifier. They were set correctly, but the rock music had lost a great deal of its appeal, and I could not zero in on that missing element.

"Just then the doorbell rang, and there stood Henry, a close buddy. 'Henry, you came to visit at the right time. Something strange is taking place, and I can't figure it out.' After pouring the rest of the last can of beer into a glass, I handed it to him. Tasting it, Henry pronounced it excellent. I told him that mine tasted less than good.

" 'Let me taste the beer in your glass; I can't believe you.' After taking a mouthful, he headed for the kitchen sink, then sputtered, 'That was putrid. Awful stuff. Man, you have a real problem here, and I can't help you. I don't want to scare you, but I believe that a supernatural force is at work here. By the way, I came to borrow one of your tools for a couple days.' "

My interest in Robert's experience was naturally mounting, and I couldn't help asking him what he thought of his friend's comment about the supernatural.

"My first thought," Robert replied, "was that someone had been praying for me and the Lord was doing something to get me to give some serious thought to my way of life. The experience kind of stunned me, and from that day on I could no longer drink beer."

As we chatted, he gave me additional details about the incident, but I was most impressed by what he described next.

"A couple days after the beer incident, I almost lost my life. It was a November evening about 8:00, and I was driving down a small hill. Since it had been raining and the road surface was beginning to freeze in spots, I had slowed down to about 35 miles per hour when suddenly four deer jumped onto the road. The headlights startled them, and they halted in the middle of the road.

"Instantly I slammed on the brakes, and the car started to spin like a top on a glass table. It kept going in circles without hitting the shoulders of the road, and continued all the way to the bottom of the hill. After the first turn, I saw that the deer had vanished, but there was no way of stopping the car. After a couple hundred feet the road was level again and the car slowed right down and came to rest sideways against a guardrail.

"It was on the driver's side of the car, and after regaining my composure, I looked over the rail with my flashlight and saw a drop of about 80 feet."

When I asked him what thoughts went through his mind when he realized that he was safe, he replied, "I felt impressed that someone's prayers had been answered. Naturally those two experiences started me thinking very seriously about the fact that someone valued my life more greatly than I did.

"It also encouraged me to return to God when I realized that while I had given up on Him, He had not abandoned me. From that time on, I found myself weighing what I was doing in this present life against the reality of eternal life. I had a lot of backtracking to do in order to get on the right road again. Drugs had a powerful hold on me, one that I knew I could not break myself. But I decided to talk the whole matter over with Jesus, and to follow as He would lead. And lead He did. Today I am a free man again, having had victory over self, over sin, and over the world."

Robert's story strengthened my prayer ministry and

helped me acquire more completely something that I had been seeking for a long time: an unfaltering trust in my heavenly Father, and in the power of His Holy Spirit.

Reflections

I don't agree with those Christian parents who assume that if their sons or daughters depart from the Lord, there isn't much that we or God can do, because the young people are exercising their freedom of choice. Such parents believe that all they can do is pray that the Lord will watch over their wayward children.

Such reasoning can have disastrous results. While it is true that God will not force the will, yet through our intercessions that claim the blood of Christ, His Spirit can overrule the forces of darkness and control events in such a way that the ones we are praying for will be helped to decide for right—even if they have to experience some suffering.

Let's consider Samson's experience. I can imagine how distressed Manoah and his wife must have been when the boy they had brought up for God began to associate with idolaters. For 20 years as he ruled Israel he kept repeating immorality. Then one day Manoah came from the city and told his wife that he had some real bad news, that she better sit down, as she would be shocked. He stated that the Philistine rulers had put out Samson's eyes while he was visiting a prostitute.

I am inclined to believe that while Mrs. Manoah felt terrible at hearing the news, she wasn't shocked to the extent of believing that God had failed them. Surely they prayed that God would somehow save Samson in His eternal kingdom, regardless of what it would take to bring their son to his senses.

In prison Samson did some serious thinking. Scene after scene of his childhood days passed before him. He turned to God with his whole heart, and in the eleventh chapter of Hebrews we read that he will stand before God someday with all other champions of faith.

CHAPTER
8

Praying for the Ungodly and the Wicked

I have seen almost unbelievable changes take place in the lives of many through intercession on their behalf. The success I have experienced over the years in my prayer ministry is totally a result of the divine outworking of God's Holy Spirit. I cannot claim any glory to myself.

We are in a fierce conflict with the powers of darkness for the control of human minds. And I have found by experience that God's Holy Spirit alone can bring victory here. To help people, I have followed the advice given on page 431 of *The Desire of Ages.*

"Earnest, persevering supplication to God in faith . . . can alone avail to bring men the Holy Spirit's aid in the battle against principalities and powers, the rulers of the darkness of this world, and wicked spirits in high places."

Through intercessory prayer I have seen the way open for God to exercise His divine grace toward most undeserving individuals. I have been greatly encouraged in praying for the ungodly and the wicked by Ellen White's statements that God rejoices to aid those who do not deserve it.

"Grace is an attribute of God exercised toward undeserving human beings. We did not seek for it, but it was sent in search of us. God rejoices to bestow His grace upon us, not because we are worthy, but because we are so utterly unworthy. Our only claim to His mercy is our great need" (*The Ministry of Healing*, p. 161).

As time went by in my work and I returned year after year to review the yellow pages advertising of my customers, and saw how the Spirit of God changed and brightened the lives of some of the ungodly persons I had been praying for, I became more excited about my prayer ministry.

I asked the Lord to lead me into a deeper prayer experience with Him, so that I could see His Spirit bless the lives of a greater number of people. It wasn't long before He answered my prayers.

By now I was in my 50s and had passed up many opportunities to get into management. But one day I concluded that the time had arrived to make a change in my occupation. Physically I was beginning to slow down, and a statement my boss had made a while back echoed in my mind: "Roger, you should give serious thought to earning your living by sharing your experience with younger men, especially when you are reaching the point where nature will no longer allow you to work such long hours."

He reminded me of a number of successful managerial experiences I had had from filling in in emergencies, such as a 1970 assignment to help the New Brunswick telephone company restructure their telephone directory operation for that Canadian province.

After having accepted the responsibility, I had suggested making many of the directories bilingual since in some areas of the Maritime Provinces the population is 50 to 75 percent Frenchspeaking. After leading the sales force for a number of weeks to get things going in the right direction, I returned to Buffalo, New York.

With the blessing of God the New Brunswick assignment turned out to be a huge success, and from that time on, upper management kept offering me managerial positions that I had declined. If I went into management, I wondered, would it hinder the Lord's blessing? Would I find myself working in my own feeble human strength? If I assumed responsibility of men who at times profaned the name of God by their language, would it affect God's ability to prosper my own work?

Many of the men that would be working under me, though cultured and well-mannered college graduates, would be lacking an experience with God. Isaiah 59:1, 2 had guided my life for many years. "Behold, the Lord's hand is not shortened, that it cannot save; neither his ear heavy, that it cannot hear: but your iniquities have separated between you and your God, and your sins have hid his face from you, that he will not hear." I wanted nothing to come between me and God.

Again and again I kept asking myself, Would the behavior of those under me raise a barrier between me and God so that He could not bless my work? I placed the matter in prayer before the Lord and asked that He would clearly answer my questions and open a clear path for me to follow.

But first I went through a couple experiences that broadened my understanding of how to remove the wall of separation that the ungodly and the wicked have erected to hide the face of God from themselves.

Shocked Into Prayer

One Friday afternoon in April as I drove home from work, I passed a F. W. Woolworth store and decided to stop and pick up a couple items that I needed. Returning to my car, I thought I might as well take a few minutes to process the day's paperwork.

The thermometer had reached into the high 70s. Getting into the car, I quickly opened the windows and let the heat out. A few minutes later a green Mercury pulled into a parking place two spaces away. Glancing out of the corner of one eye, I saw a middle-aged couple with the woman at the steering wheel.

"Mary, you will have to turn the key so that I can roll up this power window," the man said.

"Jim, you're stupid. I've told you a hundred times to roll the windows up while the engine is still running. Won't you ever learn?"

The man opened his mouth, and a flurry of profanities poured out, a mixture of the sacred and profane such as could not fail to get the message across to his wife that her words had touched a sensitive spot. Getting angrier by the moment, he accused her of having wrecked what had been a perfect day by refusing to keep her big mouth shut.

What a wicked man, I thought to myself. Then I immediately prayed, "Jesus, please forgive them. By the mighty power of Thy Holy Spirit, please rebuke the demonic forces oppressing their minds, and bless their lives with the sweet peace of Thy love."

Instantly the verbal storm stopped. For about 20 seconds neither said a word, then the man broke the silence. "Mary, I am sorry I got so angry. Really, I feel bad now that I spoke to you in the way I did. I don't know why I get so angry at times. I can actually feel anger swell up in me toward people I dearly love. Please forgive me, and I promise to put forth real effort not to repeat these outbursts."

Then it was beautiful to hear her admit that she was at least partly at fault for not being careful with her words, and at times actually took pleasure in verbally jabbing him. Promising to be more considerate in the future, she gave him a peck of a kiss, put the window up, and they both got out of the car to go shopping.

Stepping to the parking meter, the husband studied his coins to feed the meter, and having no dime or nickels, turned to his wife. "Sugar pie, would you be kind enough to look in your purse for a dime?"

"How can I refuse to help when you are treating me as a lady? Do you realize, Jim, that you haven't called me your sugar pie since the kids were little?" After he put the coins in the meter, she grabbed him by the arm, and like two newlyweds they proceeded to do some shopping.

As I sat in my car I was more than surprised over the drastic transformation that had taken place in their lives, and at the same time a new dimension had been added to my Christian experience. Never before had I asked the Lord to forgive someone. Only a sense of shock had impelled me to pray for them. When the verbal abuses started to fly, I realized that the man probably hadn't asked for his sins to be forgiven in many years. Knowing that sin separates between God and man, I sensed the urgency of the moment and asked the Lord to give both of them special help.

It amazed me to see how quickly and how differently the couple's outlook changed when the Spirit of God touched their lives. And I had been instrumental in opening the way by my intercession. The thought that during His ministry on earth Jesus carried out that kind of problem-solving now deeply impressed me.

To the paralytic who was hoping for physical healing, Jesus said, "Thy sins are forgiven thee" (Luke 5:20). First the Lord removed from the helpless man his burden of sin, then He did the next best thing, that is, heal his infirmity. At Simon's house, when a woman seeking peace for her soul anointed the Saviour's feet with expensive ointment, Jesus said, "Thy sins are forgiven; Thy faith hath saved thee; go in peace" (Luke 7:48-50).

That's it, I said to myself. My first concern in praying for the ungodly and the wicked is to ask Jesus to deal with their burdens of sin. My heart rejoiced in the fact that my Lord is an expert in salvation, specializing in hopeless cases. As I was driving home, my heart filled with thanksgiving over His infinite goodness and grace.

I prayed that if it were pleasing in His sight I would like to have another similar experience, one that would again demonstrate the power of the Holy Spirit to bless once the burden of sin has been removed.

The manager of a large lumber and building supply operation told me that it would be difficult to talk to the owner about his advertising because he owned other businesses that took him out of town a lot. The directory canvass supervisor had given me the account to handle, with the understanding that if I could not see the owner on the premises during canvass time, I could close it over the phone at a later date. After all, the man hadn't changed his advertising program for years. Besides, he had previously refused to make appointments, and seemed to run his businesses according to the way he felt on a particular day.

Because I passed in front of his place of business every day, I stopped every so often. But it was not until Monday of my last week in the area that the manager informed me that the owner desired additional advertising, and wanted to change some of the copy in his existing ads. The boss was in, but in a bad mood. "Too many things to attend to," the manager said. I asked him to get me a definite appointment to see the owner, or he would find himself having the same program in the coming telephone directory. A message left at the telephone office that afternoon indicated that the owner would see me Wednesday at 10:00 in the morning.

Wednesday was a beautiful day, and up to that time all had gone well. Entering the establishment, I found it to be a beehive of activities. Spotting the manager from a distance, I made my way to the counter, where he was serving a customer. He told a clerk to finish serving his client, and we walked up to the second floor and the owner's office.

Along the way he mentioned that it was unfortunate that I had to see the boss on this day. The man was in a really bad mood. To begin with, he had arrived with a somber expression. "Must have gotten up on the wrong side of the bed." A short while later he exploded when told that a shipment he had been promised for that day had been delayed through unexpected circumstances. "So prepare yourself for anything," the manager warned. "If the boss shouts at you, don't pay attention to him. It's probably the price he has to pay for being wealthy."

Arriving at the glassed-in office, the manager opened the door and announced me.

"Have him come in and sit down," the owner replied. "I can't talk to him right now, as I have to make a phone call."

As I entered, he didn't even look at me, but kept shuffling papers on his desk. *What a rude person he is*, I thought for a moment. Then I realized that the man was under terrible pressures. His expression reflected internal turmoil. He was undoubtedly a chain smoker, as the office was full of smoke and the ashtray with cigarette butts, and he had a cigarette between his fingers.

After dialing a number on the phone, he began talking to one of his managers in a way I wouldn't have thought possible. Only a tyrant would have used the abusive language that he blasted the man's ears with. He was unhappy about the figures shown on the quarterly report of one of his businesses. Profanities flew right and left, and the more he talked, the more brutal he seemed to get.

This fellow is disgusting—he makes me want to vomit, I thought to myself. Then the memory of my prayer a few days before struck me. Here indeed was another opportunity to pray for an ungodly person so that I could see God remove the individual's burden of sin and the Holy Spirit move with power to help that person "in the battle against principalities and powers, the rulers of the darkness of this world, and wicked spirits in high places."

Unfortunately, I had no desire to pray for him. Yes, I knew that it was the right thing to do, and I made a special effort to pray. "Dear Jesus, I need Your help. I just don't feel like praying for this wicked man. In fact, I would like to walk out of here. You have instructed us to love the unlovable, and for that reason I pray for special help now.

"Please help me to see this man not as he is now, but as he will be by Your grace on that great day when You will resurrect and translate the people of Your righteousness."

Immediately a sense of pity for the man filled my heart, and I continued to pray. "Wash away the condemnation that he has brought upon himself by his wicked deeds. Break through, I pray, the gigantic wall of separation that he has erected to hide himself from Thy face, thereby depriving himself of the sweet peace of our heavenly Father's love and grace.

"Lord, through the power of Thy Holy Spirit, please rebuke the demonic forces that may have been oppressing this man's mind, driving him to sow misery in the lives of others. And having done this, please surround him with a divine atmosphere of light and peace as Thy Spirit abides with him this day, speaking to his heart of the ways of righteousness. Thank You, Lord, for always hearing my petitions for help to the needy."

I determined there and then that this man was going to be in my daily prayers. Immediately I felt the powerful presence of the Spirit of God. I should mention here that my Christian experience has never been dependent upon my feelings, but upon a "Thus saith the Lord." At times when the going has been rough I have been tempted to believe that God has left me to carry my burden alone, but in the end I come to see how graciously the Spirit of God is watching over me. However, there have been a number of occasions when our heavenly Father especially honored me by manifesting His presence in an unmistakable way.

It wasn't more than five seconds before I witnessed a transformation in the man as great as night and day. His conversation took on a new sense of direction. Instead of talking almost continually and shouting profanities, he softened the tone of his voice and began to speak with what appeared to be intelligent reasoning. Long pauses gave the other person a chance to explain the situation. The conversation closed on what appeared to be a tensionless note, and he hung up the phone. His stern expression that had at first appeared as unchangeable as some of those seen on monuments in city parks now softened.

A smile took form as he turned toward me. "I am Dennis D," and he stood up behind his desk to extend his hand toward me in a friendly way.

"Roger Morneau here," I said as I firmly shook his hand.

"It's nice meeting you, Roger. It's too bad that you happened to come on a day when everything is running rough."

Then he corrected himself. "I shouldn't be giving you the impression that the conversation you have just witnessed is a rare occurrence. To be honest with you, I must admit that I am—I am at times a madman. I am not crazy or deranged in any way, but there is something strange here. I can't understand why I get so steamed up at times over things that no one has any power to change. And such incidents seem to be more frequent and powerful as time passes. Too often I feel an uncontrollable anger building up within, and I lash out at everybody."

I could tell that the man was deeply distressed by his situation. "If it weren't for the fact that I pay my managers twice as much as they are worth, none of them would work for me." Suddenly he realized that he was talking to a complete stranger. "What am I doing, telling you the secrets of my life? Please excuse me for dumping my problems on you. Let's talk advertising."

"Mr. D, please relax, and trust me," I said. "The very first requirement of my job is to keep in strict confidence whatever my advertisers tell me, and I have successfully done that for years. Quite frequently people tell me things they have told no one else, stating that they feel comfortable in my presence, and believe that it is better to open one's heart to a stranger than to someone who knows them well."

His reply surprised me some, as it was totally unexpected. "Roger, I agree with what your customers say. I can feel a power accompanying you that I don't know exactly how to explain, except to say that it is out of this world. I have never before experienced the peace and quiet that I do now."

"Thank you, sir, for telling me that. Mr. D, I feel that it is important for me to add that from the moment you began talking over the phone, I turned my heart in prayer to the great Monarch of the galaxies, the Life-giver, asking that He would bless your life with the presence of His Spirit that alone can bring peace and help to those in this world."

He studied me for a moment, then said, "I gave up on religion and God a long time ago. But today you have given me something to think about: the Monarch of the galaxies and His power to touch people's lives in a meaningful way. I like that thought. Don't get me wrong. I am not thinking of going to church or anything like that, but would you be kind enough to keep me in your prayers? I sure would appreciate that."

After I assured him that I would be honored to add his name to my prayer list, we then updated his advertising program. As I got up to leave, he said, "Let me walk down with you, as I have to go downstairs anyway."

On the way, I asked him how he had built such a fine business operation. His face lit up, and he told stories all the way to the front door. Shaking my hand as we parted, he asked if I would be kind enough to see him at the beginning of the telephone directory canvass the following year.

I did not work the directory that year, but I found myself visiting the area two years later as division sales manager, and went on that call with the fellow who had the account. The man was delighted to see me again and was very courteous, and while a new ad was being set up, he had me walk with him to another office to meet his accountant.

After introducing us, he stated that I was the person who had given him a new lease on life, and at the same time saved him a bundle of money, as he no longer ha⁻¹ any need "to see his shrink."

A great transformation had taken place in that individual's life. He was vibrant with the joy of living. On the wall in back of his desk hung a lovely plaque with "Prayer changes things" inscribed on it.

Indeed it does—and in this particular instance, I am inclined to believe that of all the blessings received, I was the greater beneficiary of the two of us. That prayer experience had straightened out my warped reasoning that for a number of years had kept me from asking for special help for the ungodly. But from that time on, the Lord was able to use me to open the way so that His Spirit could then move in a marvelous manner to benefit the lives of many others.

9

Every Problem a Call to Prayer

As division sales manager of the Northeast Division, covering a geographical area of eight states, I spent most of my time visiting telephone directory canvasses in progress.

Looking over several weekly sales reports, I decided to visit our yellow pages salespeople working on a major directory in Pennsylvania. One man's sales results in particular had caught my attention. Previously a top achiever, he was now experiencing a substantial loss of revenue. I concluded that Charles had a problem that interfered with his work.

Conversing with him, I found that his ex-wife, who had custody of their two children, was making it difficult for him to see their children. In addition, his ex-mother-in-law was doing everything possible to turn the children against him, which just about broke his heart. He admitted that he had a hard time keeping his mind on his work, and that if things didn't improve soon, he would have to quit his job.

I asked for the mother-in-law's name so that I could pray for her. He was a bit surprised by my request, but gave it after commenting that "I doubt that prayers will help, seeing that my parents have been praying for the old witch from the day I married her daughter. In fact, they even had a couple of Masses celebrated so that she would not break up our home, and that didn't help."

To make a long story short, I placed the names of the

ex-wife, ex-mother-in-law, and the kids on my prayer list along with that of Charles, and every morning, with my Bible open at the twenty-seventh chapter of Matthew, I interceded in their behalf. And above all I prayed that the Spirit of God would help Charles carry his burdens without falling apart.

It was company procedure that all yellow pages representatives would phone the division office in Virginia on Friday between 1:00 and 3:00 in the afternoon to report their figures for the week completed. They stated the amount of advertising dollars handled, the decrease or loss, the net figure, and any changes in number of advertisers.

As I traveled home on Friday, I would stop after 3:00 and phone the office to get the sales results of the men that needed my close attention. It was extremely encouraging, and at the same time a blessing to my Christian experience, to get Charles's figures and see how the Spirit of God was blessing, guiding, directing, and encouraging him as those sales results improved from week to week.

Sometime later I heard all about it from the man himself. With a joy born of heaven, he told how things were changing for the better. He said a couple times, "Your prayers have real power. They really work for people."

While company policies prevented me from talking religion with my people, I was able to live my religious convictions, and I thank God for that. I was surprised to hear one of their comments about living my religion. Because of a health problem, a rep's doctor told him that he had to move to a warm climate. Before leaving for California, he came to see my wife and me. To my great surprise, he told Hilda in my presence about the high regard my associates had for me. "One fellow stated that the day he begins going to church again, he will go to Roger's church. He will become an SDA and belong to a church that has power."

A Liquor Problem Solved

George was a good worker, but on weekends he usually rewarded himself for a job well done by drinking. A single man, he lived in Boston, but one weekend had stayed in a New England city where he was working on the telephone directory.

On Friday evening he drank too much and somehow landed in jail. He called the manager of the telephone company, who bailed him out. The next morning after having sobered up, he figured that he should not delay in trying to save his job.

He thought of calling me, but assumed that I, being a Seventh-day Adventist and a religious person, would likely fire him on the spot. Instead he called the division office in Virginia with the hope that he might be able to talk to my boss, whom he presumed would be more compassionate since the man was a social drinker. My superior told George that I made those kind of decisions, and that I would be at the telephone office on Monday to discuss the matter with him.

On Sunday evening my boss phoned me at home, told about the problem, and suggested that on Monday I call a meeting of our people working the directory and, in the presence of everyone, fire the man.

Having prayed about the matter, I decided against such a move, and talked to George in private. As I traveled to the office I prayed for wisdom to handle the situation with tact. In fact, I felt that maybe I should keep him in our employ, and use his problem for a prayer experience. I believed that the Spirit of God would give the man victory over his drinking by my interceding for him. That is, if the Spirit of God would first cause him to plead with sincerity for his job.

Then I thought, *George is too proud a man to humble himself to the point of pleading for his job. He'll turn in the company materials and quit before he does that* .

However, I found the man highly distressed over his problem. As I listened to his request for compassion, I realized that he was fighting a real battle against liquor.

A quotation from *The Desire of Ages* came to mind. "Earnest, persevering supplication to God in faith . . . can alone avail to bring men the Holy Spirit's aid in the battle against principalities and powers, the rulers of the darkness of this world, and wicked spirits in high places" (p. 431).

It was with tears in his eyes that he finally said, "Please give me another chance! Please!"

"George," I replied, "another chance I am giving you. But

seeing that I am sticking my neck out for you, I am going to help you in giving up liquor by praying that God will bless your life and give you victory over your drinking."

Thanking me, he said, "However, I don't think that prayers will help. My mother has been praying for 15 years over my problem. She has recited the rosary and paid to have Masses celebrated so that I would get victory over the problem, but it has not helped."

"Well, George, I believe in miracles, so let's see what will happen."

That's exactly what did take place—a miracle brought about by God's Holy Spirit. A few months later he told me how delighted he was that he had given up drinking. He had lost all sense of pleasure from his drinking.

I wish to again make a point very clear: while the Holy Spirit doesn't force a person's will, He can do a lot to change a person's course of action in answer to persevering supplications to God in faith.

Putting on the Brakes

After attending a managers' meeting at the home office in Kansas City, I returned to the Northeast Division with a new objective in mind: to reduce the high turnover of yellow pages advertising salespeople in our division.

At the airport as we waited for my flight to take off, I conversed with two other division sales managers about the concept. They felt that for the vice president of sales to attempt such a thing was ridiculous. It would mean making all our people top producers, they said, and that couldn't be done. Many reps had problems at home that forced them to quit their work. Others, though well-intentioned and hard workers, just didn't have what it took to be successful. So there was only one thing to do, they argued—keep putting new people through training school, costly though that might be. There was no other way.

As for myself, I already knew that with the Holy Spirit blessing my people and their advertising customers, remarkable improvements could be made. Charles's experience along with George's had already proved that.

Some time went by, and on a Thursday evening my boss called me from Kansas. I had been at the Holiday Inn in Lowell, Massachusetts, for three days interviewing sales applicants referred to us by the Snelling and Snelling Employment Agency. "How many men will you have in next month's training class in Kansas City?" he immediately asked.

"As things now stand," I replied, "there will be no one attending."

After a long pause, he inquired, "Aren't you going to replace the three fellows that are trailing at the back of the sales force, the new fellows you and I talked about last week?"

"At the time of our conversation I was leaning in that direction, but today I am thinking differently. Boss, please excuse the analogy, but I have come to the conclusion that this business of letting people go after they have been with us for five months simply because they have not produced great results is a bit ridiculous. It's like acquiring thoroughbreds, casting them aside if they don't win a major race in the first year, and then turning around and buying more of the same.

"Believe me, sir, none of the people I have been talking to this week have impressed me as being better than the fellows we now have. If it's OK with you, I would like to keep the three, spend some time with them in the field, and try to make our present investments pay off."

"I am delighted to hear you talk that way. You know that I am progress-minded."

"If you recall, at our last managers' meeting the vice president of sales stated that it costs our company about $5,000 to have a man in school for a month and in the field for five months. What I would like to do—if it meets with your approval—is to try saving some of that $5,000. What do you say?"

"I don't understand exactly how you are going to make top producers out of those three, but I sure would like to see you try. I am with you 100 percent, but I must tell you that if you proceed that way, you are going to step on the toes of the national sales manager, and you may make yourself an enemy.

He has established a top-notch training school on the premise that a lot of high-caliber people going through its doors are needed to obtain a large percentage of top producers."

"I can't see why he would be unhappy with the vice president of sales encouraging us to try reducing the high turnover."

"He shouldn't, but he will if you are successful, because you will have started a trend that will jeopardize the future of his school."

"I appreciate your telling me about this," I said, "but I will not let it change my plans."

"Now we have another problem. He is expecting to have 35 men in the coming class. I have already notified him of our plans to have three recruits attending. But tomorrow morning I will tell him of your decision. Prepare yourself for a telephone call from Roy before the day is over."

I had placed my plans before the Lord and felt impressed that I was going in the right direction, and determined to let no one change my mind. But you can rest assured that I spent a lot of time praying for those fellows. The next three weeks I spent with them in the field, one week for each man. I went with them on all their business calls, and to pleasantly surprise them, during the first two days I handled all calls myself.

I placed them into such a relaxed state of mind that they found the experience a real pleasure. We chatted about a great many things, enabling me to learn much about their homes, the members of their families, etc. The men felt that they had benefited highly from the experience, which served to encourage them and produced good sales results. I believe that the Spirit of God had led me in that direction so that I could have the privilege of bringing the rich blessings of God into their homes through my intercessory prayers.

My prayer list grew longer and longer as I got to know my people better. And the time came when I didn't even turn the radio on in my car for the news, but spent all my traveling time interceding in prayer for someone. I should add that of the five divisions of Continental Telephone, the Northeast Division became known as the division with the lowest turnover of yellow pages representatives in the entire nation.

My boss often told the higher-ups that I was the man that had the power to put the brakes on and bring the turnover of our sales force in the Northeast Division to a solid stop. While he gave me the recognition, he knew that the power came from above. I made doubly sure that he understood that.

At the time that I was made district sales manager the Northeast Division was the least productive of all the divisions. But because of the blessings of God, in a few short years we reached the top. In 1977 my boss and I were awarded the Masters Circle Award for our division's coming in first place for that year, excelling in all phases of company operations.

From then on to the time that I left the company in 1981, our division had the lowest turnover of salespeople and stood at the top in all other company objectives except for net increase to advertisers. (The Pacific Division, because of the phenomenal prosperity of the state of California, held that honor.)

Afterward

As I have shared with you in this book, God has answered many of my prayers for others. Many more He could not. Praying for others has been the special calling and spiritual gift He has given me in His service. God works differently in each person's life, however. Most of the time He answers our prayers in less spectacular ways than those I have recorded here. But He awaits for the prayers of all of His children. He longs that each one of us will pray for those about us. May you, my readers, take some of the principles I have found in my own experience, and with the power of the Holy Spirit use them to know the God-given joy of interceding in prayer for others.